MW01229979

A POEM A DAY

TO PRAY

2025

Medard Laz

ALSO BY MEDARD LAZ

Lift Up My Spirit, Lord!

The Six Levels of a Happy Marriage

Life After the Divorce

Coping When Your Spouse Dies

Spiritual Guidance for the Separated and Divorced

After Your Loved One Dies

Parenting After Divorce

Making Parish Meetings Work

Love Adds a Little Chocolate

The Gathering, Jesus and Abortion, A Story for Our Time

A POEM A DAY

TO PRAY

2025

Medard Laz

MEDARD LAZ

HFH PUBLISHERS
Hearts for Humanity, Inc.
3015 N. Ocean Blvd. 18H
Fort Lauderdale, FL 33308

HFH Hardcopy and Digital Edition 2025 Library of Congress
Cataloging-in-Publication Data has been applied for.

International Standard Book Number:
ISBN: 9798342242714
Printed in the United States of America

Cover Design by
Medard Laz & Tim Veach

To all those who have been a beacon of light to me in my darkest times, igniting a dormant spark in me. You showed me rainbows every time I saw the rain.

To all those who helped me emerge as a butterfly when I was a caterpillar crawling on the ground. You taught me to fly.

To all those who were a gust of wind on my many stagnant days. You came into my life and blew me away.

Soren Kierkegaard, the renowned Danish theologian, philosopher, and poet, was once asked, *"What is a poet?*

His answer: *"A poet is an unhappy person who conceals deep torments in his or her heart, but whose lips are so formed that when a groan or shriek streams over them it sounds like beautiful music."*

I hope you find that my efforts along with help from Artificial Intelligence at times sound like beautiful music.

Wednesday, January 1, 2025

New Year's Day

GIVE THANKS TO GOD FOR A NEW YEAR

We give thanks to God for a New Year's start,
With hope and faith in every heart.
Eternal optimists, through and through,
We trust this year brings something new.

Last year's trials, left behind,
We look ahead with an open mind.
None can say what days will bring,
Yet, with Christ, our spirits sing.

Remember, dear ones, who we are,
And what we can become, near or far.
With Christ within, our souls take flight,
Designed for greatness, shining bright.

An angel or a saint within us hides,
Yearning to break forth, to be our guide.
This coming year, let's set them free,
To live with love and humility.

May our journey be unforgettably blessed,
For with a living Jesus, we find our best.
In every moment, His presence near,
Guiding us through another year.

YOUR PROBLEMS HAVE AN EXPIRATION DATE. THEY
WON'T LAST FOREVER. GOD'S PROMISES NEVER EXPIRE.
THEY WILL STAND FOREVER!

OUR NEW YEAR 2025

In 2025 I will strive to make each day an Amen.
To cherish each moment like a precious gem.
In every act, I'll seek a real delight,
And bask in warmth, from morn til night.

I'll aim to be gracious, warm, and kind,
With an open heart and an open mind.
I'll welcome love more than before,
Leaving past hurts at the door.

I'll keep my humor through the fight,
And find courage in the darkest night.
No longer will I count what's lost,
But treasure life, despite the cost.

With God's love lighting up my way,
I'll embrace the dawn of every day.
In every breath, in every plan,
I'll find the joy in who I am.

For life is full, and life is grand,
Ever blessed by God's gentle hand.
With love to guide me from above,
I'll live this life with faith and love

DON'T JUST COUNT YOUR BLESSINGS, BE THE BLESSING
OTHER PEOPLE COUNT ON!

Friday, January 3, 2025

AN UNSEEN FORCE IN WHAT WE SAY

We carry with us, day by day,
An unseen force in what we say.
Our presence brings a certain light,
Or casts a shadow, dull or bright.

When we walk into a crowded space,
The energy we leave, takes its place.
If filled with joy, with love and grace,
That spirit lingers in every face.

But if we bring a darker shade,
With anger, fear, or lies we've made,
That energy, though words may bend,
Will leave behind a bitter end.

The spirit left when we depart,
Remains within each mind and heart.
It colors all that lingers still,
A silent echo, strong or ill.

So may we strive to leave behind,
A presence warm, sincere, and kind.
For what we give in every way,
Will live in hearts beyond our stay.

IF YOU WANT GOD TO CLOSE AND OPEN DOORS FOR
YOU, THEN LET GO OF THE DOOR KNOB!

"I'LL PRAY FOR YOU!"

"I'll pray for you!" we often say,
But do we trust in what we pray?
Can words alone change what we fear,
Or bring the distant loved ones near?

Can prayers move mountains, heal the ill,
Stop pandemics, and bend God's will?
When life is tough and hope seems thin,
Can prayer bring light, new strength within?

We wonder what inspires a change,
What makes the world rearrange.
Is it pure luck or just a chance,
Or do our prayers direct the dance?

A leader's heart that finds its grace,
A softened gaze, a kinder face.
A scientist whose mind alights,
To find a cure in darkest nights.

In every prayer, we touch the sky,
In every plea, we question why.
Perhaps in faith, we find the key,
That prayer does more than we can see.

GOD IS ALWAYS WITH YOU.....YOU JUST NEED TO PAY
ATTENTION!

Sunday, January 5, 2025

Epiphany Sunday

THE WISE MEN FOLLOWED THE STAR

The Wise Men followed the star so bright,
A beacon of hope in the darkest night.
Their journey long, with thoughts profound,
Seeking Jesus where love is found.

Many Herods lurked along their path,
With schemes and wiles, their hearts of wrath.
But faith and wisdom led the way,
Through doubt and fear, they did not sway.

For Christians, a star is more than light,
It's guidance pure in the darkest night.
To follow where God's whispers lead,
Beyond the temptations, beyond the greed.

Herods try to block our quest,
Addictions, tempers, all life's test.
But the Wise Men taught us, clear and true,
With faith and courage, we can break through.

They went home by another way,
Their hearts transformed, forever to stay.
For once you've found Jesus, pure and bright,
You cannot return to the old, dark night.

YOU ARE NOT ON A JOURNEY <u>TO</u> GOD, YOU ARE ON A
JOURNEY <u>WITH</u> GOD!

Monday, January 6, 2025

A BEACON OF LOVE

There are many stars and lights that twinkle bright,
Guiding us through the darkness of night.
We must choose wisely the ones to follow,
For some lights are fleeting, leaving us hollow.

Flashing lights come and go, pleasures so brief,
Good in the moment, but they offer no relief.
They do not last, nor give lasting cheer,
Their joy fades quickly, leaving us here.

The dazzling lights of money and success,
Promise so much, in their grand excess.
Seductive and bright, they capture our sight,
But their blinding glare fades into the night.

The Three Wise Men invite us to see,
A steady light that guides you and me.
Where does it shine? In our hearts so true,
Guiding our steps in all that we do.

So choose the light that leads to peace,
A beacon of love that will never cease.
In its glow, find unending joy and delight,
For it shines forever, through the darkest night.

THIS IS THE DRESSING ROOM FOR ETERNITY. IN THE FEW
FLEETING DAYS OF LIFE ON THIS PLANET YOU ARE
GIVEN THE OPPORTUNITY TO PREPARE FOR ETERNITY!

PRAYER ISN'T EASY

Prayer isn't easy; it's hard to find
A quiet place, a settled mind.
We're tired, distracted, minds askew,
Yet in this chaos, I turn to You.

No matter how my day has been,
Amidst the noise, the rush, the din,
I find a moment, still and small,
To pray the prayer You gave us all.

The Our Father, simple, true,
I offer up my words to You.
In times of strength, in moments weak,
I ask for peace, for the love that I seek.

It's not much, just a whispered plea,
From deep within my frailty.
And though my mind might wander wide,
I know God's love is by my side.

Each day I come, as best I can,
To speak the words You taught to man.
In this small act, I find my way,
To touch Your grace, if just for today.

DON'T FORGET TO PRAY TODAY.....BECAUSE GOD DIDN'T
FORGET TO WAKE YOU UP THIS MORNING!

WE THINK WE HOLD THE REINS OF LIFE

We think we hold the reins of life,
To guard ourselves from pain and strife.
In strength, we trust, in might, we stand,
Believing safety's in our hand.

We hate the cracks, the flaws we bear,
Our weakness is a weight we wear.
We yearn for power, to feel secure,
To be invulnerable, and so mature.

This pride, is a grace that keeps us sane,
Protects our hearts from endless pain.
Yet deep within, a truth we find,
That shatters peace within our mind.

For deep within, we know the truth,
Our grip on life is not aloof.
In moments clear, our hearts confess,
We need each other's tenderness.

We're meant to know we're not alone,
Our strength comes not from us alone.
In God, we trust, in love, we find,
That we're interdependent, intertwined.

WHEN YOU GET TO YOUR WIT'S END, YOU'LL FIND THAT
GOD LIVES THERE!

Thursday, January 9, 2025

GOD IS HAPPY

God is happy, how could God not be?
In perfect goodness, full and free.
In truth and beauty, joy abides,
In every heart, His love resides.

In perfect joy, God stands complete,
For happiness in God is sweet.
No lack, no loss, no hint of woe,
A perfect joy no end can know.

Yet does God frown when we go astray?
Or sigh in sorrow at our way?
Though sin may darken our bright earth,
His love remains, of constant worth.

Like a parent guiding a child's first steps,
God leads with joy, not harsh regrets.
God understands our fragile hearts,
And in our growth, His joy imparts.

For God is happy, ever true,
Delighting in the good we do.
God lures us forward, lifts our gaze,
With endless love, for all our days.

GOD IS THE ONLY ONE WHO CAN LOVE EVERYTHING
YOU ARE DESPITE EVERYTHING YOU'RE NOT!

GOD'S GRACE WILL LIFT US

Sometimes in struggles, strength will rise,
Buried deep beneath our cries.
From wounds we heal, and walk once more,
With health and hope we do restore.

But other times, the pain's too deep,
A broken heart that cannot leap.
We feel as if our life's been lost,
A shattered soul, too high the cost.

In those dark times when hope seems gone,
When strength within cannot be drawn,
Remember there's a deeper grace,
A love that fills the empty space.

For when our hearts can't bear the load,
And life feels like a heavy road,
God's grace will lift us from the fall,
His love's the strength that holds us all.

No wound too deep, no pain too great,
For in God's heart, there is no fate.
His love's a balm for every scar,
A light that shines, no matter how far.

GOD MADE THE WORLD ROUND SO WE WOULD NEVER BE
ABLE TO SEE TOO FAR DOWN THE ROAD!

GIVE YOURSELF PERMISSION TO FEEL

Give yourself permission to feel,
The restlessness that's raw and real.
For chaos lives within the soul,
No matter how you seek control.

We often think that peace should reign,
That calm should come and still the pain.
But hearts, complex and deeply true,
Will ache and yearn for something new.

No life's immune to inner strife,
No perfect peace in human life.
The sensitive will feel it more,
The pull of something yet in store.

We try to mute what stirs inside,
With fleeting joys or busy pride.
But, Lord, our hearts can't find their due,
Until they find their rest in You.

There's no complete, harmonious way,
To end this longing, come what may.
The symphony remains unplayed,
Till Heaven calls and fears are allayed.

GOD'S WORD IS NOT JUST TO BE HEARD AND REPEATED.
IT IS TO BE BREATHED, LIVED AND EMULATED WITH
EACH OF YOUR ACTIONS!

Sunday, January 12, 2025

THE BAPTISM OF JESUS

Many have said that Jesus went to the Jordan river,
Not for His sins, but to decide what to deliver.
He was ready at thirty to begin His call,
Leaving the carpenter's life for one that served us all.

In the Jordan with John, a new path was revealed,
From private to public, His purpose unsealed.
Whether baptized as a child or as an adult anew,
It's a time for decision, a life to pursue.

Are we like Jesus, a person for others?
Or wrapped in ourselves, ignoring our brothers?
Baptism calls us to choose our direction,
A life of service or just self-reflection?

To live like Jesus, selfless and kind,
Is to leave selfish desires behind.
To embrace the world with open hands,
And fulfill the purpose that God commands.

So let us decide, with hearts open wide,
To walk with compassion, and not turn aside.
In every choice, let love be our guide,
Living for others, in whom we abide.

WE NEED JESUS TO MAKE US FEEL LIKE TOMORROW IS
MORE THAN JUST ANOTHER DAY!

POWER ISN'T JUST IN MIGHT

There's power in strength, a force untamed,
In muscles flexed, and bodies trained.
The athlete moves with grace and might,
Commanding awe with every flight.

There's power in the rock star's song,
In crowds that chant and sing along.
Charisma lights the room aglow,
A force of wills, an ebb and a flow.

But there's another power still,
A kind of strength that's soft and still.
The helpless cry, the baby's coo,
Can melt a heart and change a view.

For power isn't just in might,
It's found in hearts that hold the light.
The helpless babe, without defense,
Can change the world with just a glance.

So when you see the strong, the grand,
Remember where true powers stand.
In softness lies the greatest force,
A love that changes every course.

DEAR GOD, PLEASE INTERRUPT WHATEVER I AM DOING
TODAY SO THAT I CAN JOIN YOU IN WHAT YOU ARE
DOING!

OUR SOULS ARE SOFT

Deep within, where light is dim,
A tender voice, a sacred hymn.
Our souls, so fragile, pure, and true,
Cry out for care from me and you.

Our souls are soft, they seek our care,
They cannot guard themselves from wear.
We need to hold them with respect,
To honor all that they reflect.

Like Moses on that hallowed ground,
We must approach without a sound.
With reverence, let us stand in awe,
For in our souls, we see God's law.

We need to hear their silent pleas,
Their whispered dreams, their urgent needs.
In sorrow, joy, in fear, in fight,
Our souls speak truth both day and night.

So guard your soul with tender care,
Its voice is precious, pure, and rare.
For in its depths, life's meaning lies,
A treasure hidden from careless eyes.

THE MORE I LOOK BACK.....THE MORE I SEE MIRACLES!

GOD BREAKS INTO OUR LIVES UNKNOWN

God breaks into our lives unknown,
Through strangers, paths we've never shown.
In foreign things that catch our eye,
And plans we make that go awry.

Revelation wears a strange disguise,
It comes to us as a real surprise.
It flips our thoughts, our hearts confound,
And turns our world upside down.

For centuries they prayed with might,
For a messiah dressed in light.
They sought a king to conquer all,
But they got a baby in a stall.

God's wisdom shatters what we see,
It shows us truths we must set free.
So when a stranger comes your way,
An angel might have come to stay.

Expect the unexpected guest,
For in that surprise, we're truly blessed.
God's voice is heard in ways so odd,
Revealing love, and the heart of God.

A GRATEFUL HEART IS A MAGNET FOR MIRACLES!

THE COMFORTS THAT WE HELD SO DEAR

As age comes on, the mind grows still,
Old ways of knowing lose their thrill.
The heart, once wounded, looks ahead,
Beyond the pains it used to dread.

The comforts that we held so dear,
With time and loss, they disappear.
Our certainties all fade away,
And in their place, a different day.

This light, it calls, both strange and new,
A glow that brings the world to view.
The past slips by, the future's veiled,
And what once mattered now seems paled.

Like a child, reborn, we stand,
Our minds can't grasp or understand.
Silent now, we gaze in awe,
At all the mysteries we once saw.

In this light, a call to trust,
To let old ways turn into dust.
We find a peace, a quiet night,
And stare into that gentle light.

SOMETIMES YOU THINK YOU ARE BEING BURIED, WHEN
YOU'RE REALLY BEING PLANTED. GOD IS USING THIS
SEASON TO GROW YOU!

Friday, January 17, 2025

THE JOYFUL HEART OF GOD

Joy is the sign of God within,
A sacred light where life can grin.
For God is joy, serene and bright,
The source of laughter, pure delight.

We often think of God as stern,
A distant force, with much concern.
But joy is woven in God's heart,
A love that laughter does impart.

If all that's good comes from God's hand,
Then joy must flow from all God planned.
The laughter, smiles, and merry cheer,
Are signs that God is always near.

How could it be that the joy we find,
Is separate from God's own mind?
For every laugh and gentle cheer,
Must spring from God who holds us near.

So let us see God as He is,
A joyful heart, a loving bliss.
For in His joy, we find our own,
A happiness that God has shown.

GOD'S PEACE IS JOY RESTING. GOD'S JOY IS PEACE
DANCING!

THE ACHE FOR GOD

A restlessness is inside everything
As the universe itself takes wing.
An ache for God within the soul,
Through every atom, that makes us whole.

The human heart, alive with fire,
Shares with the stars a deep desire.
In stones and trees, in beasts that roam,
The same pull guides them towards a home.

A yearning in each molecule,
A force that makes the planets pull.
From galaxies to drops of rain,
A shared heartache that can't be tamed.

In every leaf that bends and sways,
And in the lion's mighty gaze,
God's call resounds through earth and skies,
Uniting all with unseen ties.

For spirit, flesh, and matter blend,
As all creation seeks its end.
No boundary splits what God has drawn,
The pull towards love that leads us on.

WHY WISH UPON A STAR WHEN YOU CAN PRAY TO THE
ONE WHO CREATED IT!

Sunday, January 19, 2025

JESUS SPOKE TO YOUNG AND OLD

Jesus spoke to young and old,
A single truth, his teachings told.
No separate words for a different day,
But one clear path, a single way.

At seven, we hear with youthful ears,
The words of love, the end of fears.
At twenty-seven, the cross feels near,
A path of hope, yet tinged with fear.

In mid-life, challenges arise,
His teachings seen through wiser eyes.
The parables now speak of grace,
Of second chances we must embrace.

"Take up your cross," the call he gave,
To young and old, to wise and brave.
At different times, it stings the heart,
But guides each soul to do its own part.

His teachings stand, forever true,
Though we may age, they still renew.
For Christ's own call does not divide,
It guides us all, through life's long ride.

JESUS WAS AN EXTREMIST FOR TRUTH, LOVE AND
GOODNESS!

Monday, January 20, 2025

Martin Luther King Jr. Day

THE WEAPON OF LOVE

Dr. King, a beacon so bright,
Spoke of love, against the night.
"We'll counter force with a soul so pure,
Hate with love, our hearts secure."

At Jesus' core, His life, His call,
To make peace, to heal us all.
Violence, King said, brings no peace,
It creates more woes, they never cease.

"An eye for eye leaves all men blind,"
A path to darkness, ill-designed.
Immoral, for it breeds disdain,
A cycle of never-ending pain.

It thrives on hate, destroys the heart,
Tears our communities apart.
Violence ends in its defeat,
Leaves bitterness and much deceit.

Love alone can break this chain,
Heal the wounds, ease the pain.
In every act, in every word,
Let the call to love be heard.

JESUS DIDN'T HAVE TO AGREE WITH PEOPLE TO BE KIND
TO THEM!

Tuesday, January 21, 2025

GOD IS ONE

God is One, no split, no strife,
The source of order, truth, and life.
In God, no contradiction lies,
A constant light that never dies.

What's done is done, forever sealed,
The truth of life is thus revealed.
Two plus two will always be,
A proof of God's consistency.

To deny a fact is to lose sight,
Of what is real, of what is right.
Lies distort the world we know,
Shaking truths we need to grow.

For God's the ground where reason stands,
A stable rock, not shifting sands.
Honesty is always our guiding light,
In a world where truth leads to a fight.

God is one, and so must we,
Live in truth, both bold and free.
In honesty, we touch the divine,
In every fact, God's light will shine.

IMAGINE HOW IT WOULD CHANGE YOUR WORLD, IF YOU
DIDN'T LOOK UP TO HEAVEN FOR GOD, BUT YOU SAW
GOD IN THE FACE OF YOUR NEIGHBOR!

A SYMPHONY IN UNSEEN WAYS

Our names won't shine in neon lights,
Nor grace the news on sleepless nights.
We'll live our lives in quiet ways,
Unseen by most, through humble days.

We watch the world from far outside,
As others rise with boastful pride.
Yet in the shadows where we stay,
A deeper purpose finds its way.

Our talents bloom where few can see,
In private homes, anonymously.
Though overlooked by those who lead,
Our lives still plant a vital seed.

But in our hearts, a music plays,
A symphony in unseen ways.
A melody that's rich and pure,
That sings of lives both small and sure.

For deep within, we find our worth,
In simple acts, in love's soft birth.
Though fame and fortune pass us by,
Our quiet lives still touch the sky.

GOD TEACHES US TO LOVE BY PUTTING SOME
UNLOVELY PEOPLE AROUND US TO LIKE, AND EVEN TO
LOVE!

Thursday, January 23, 2025

WE LONG TO SURRENDER TO LOVE

We long to surrender, to give in to love,
To feel its embrace, soft as a dove.
Yet deep within, we fight and resist,
The very thing our hearts have missed.

Why do we wrestle, fight, and hide,
When love's the thing we crave inside?
Our deepest wish is to give in,
Yet fear of loss keeps us within.

We strive to prove we're worthy and strong,
In all our battles, we've fought for so long.
But in the struggle, if truth we see,
It's love itself, as we fight to be free.

A light will dawn, and we'll understand,
We're not here to conquer, but to take love's hand.
The thing we fear, the thing we fight,
Is what we've desired in the deepest night.

In the end, it's not a defeat we face,
But a surrender to love's warm embrace.
Our strength gives way, and then we find,
The love we've chased was always kind.

I'M IN A CHAPTER OF MY LIFE WHERE GOD IS MAKING
ME STRONG BEFORE MAKING ME HAPPY!

GOD CALLS EACH SOUL

God calls each soul with a whispered plea,
Not by our gifts, but our frailty,
Our talents shine, yet truly bloom,
When touched by scars and given room.

In wounds, a healer's heart is born,
A tender touch where pain has worn.
The gifts we hold, though bright and fair,
Find purpose when they're worn with care.

The world may praise the gifted strong,
Yet wounds can teach where they belong.
For gifts alone can sometimes hide,
But wounds bring forth compassion's tide.

A broken heart, a scarred past,
Can guide a soul to heal at last.
 For empathy is born from pain,
A kindness flowing like gentle rain.

Our wounds shape gifts, a healing art,
To touch the world with a humble heart.
For in your wounds, you'll find the key,
To heal the world and set it free.

SOMEDAY GOD WILL NOT LOOK YOU OVER FOR MEDALS,
DEGREES AND PORTFOLIOS. GOD WILL LOOK YOU OVER
FOR SCARS!

THE RICH GROW RICHER

The rich grow richer every day,
While the poor are cast further away.
The powerful rise, their grip so tight,
The weak are lost, and out of sight.

Inequality now rules so many lands,
With hardened hearts and calloused hands.
Wealth's embrace leaves others cold,
The poor dismissed, their worth unsold.

In God's name, this is justified,
While justice weeps, her hands are tied.
The poor, disposable, cast aside,
Their voices silenced, their dreams denied.

For women too, this truth remains,
Their rights diminished, bound in chains.
A world that prizes wealth and might,
Ignores their plea, dismisses plight.

But wealth that thrives on others' pain,
Will face its end, it can't sustain.
For every soul, both rich and poor,
Deserves a world that's just and sure.

IF YOUR INVESTMENTS ARE LIMITED TO THIS EARTH,
YOU ARE THE WORLD'S WORST INVESTOR!

Sunday, January 26, 2025

THE POWER OF FORGIVENESS

With Jesus, forgiveness is the key,
The virtue that sets our spirits free.
Without it, heaven cannot start,
We must forgive with an open heart.

 He taught us in the prayer He gave,
Forgive, if your soul you wish to save.
For if we hold on to hate and pain,
God's own mercy can't remain.

The table set in heaven's land,
Is open to those who understand,
That hearts must soften, grudges cease,
To join the feast of endless peace.

God's love invites, but we decide,
To let our hearts be open wide.
Without forgiveness, we remain apart,
From God's embrace, from heaven's heart.

So let go of anger, let it part,
And welcome peace into your heart.
For without forgiveness, life is lost,
But with it, joy is worth the cost.

JESUS, PLEASE KEEP YOUR ARM AROUND MY SHOULDER
AND YOUR HAND OVER MY MOUTH!

Monday, January 27, 2025

THE CRY OF SADNESS

Sadness comes, an uninvited guest,
A weight that sits upon our chest.
Yet in its voice, a truth does ring,
A chance for our soul's song to sing.

In sadness, we hear a silent cry,
A truth that speaks, that doesn't lie.
A loss or pain, a heart laid bare,
Life's bitter taste, a cross to bear.

Acceptance is the price we pay,
For truths that darkness cannot sway.
When sadness knocks, we must allow,
To feel its ache and learn somehow.

For in each heart, there's fragile ground,
Where love was lost or never found.
Each one of us will face our share,
Of seasons dark and burdens rare.

Sadness is the soul's own plea,
To honor loss, to set it free.
And when we listen, and hear its call,
We find the strength to face it all.

WHEN YOU RUN ALONE, IT'S CALLED A RACE. WHEN
GOD RUNS WITH YOU, IT'S CALLED GRACE!

Tuesday, January 28, 2025

AS TIME MOVES ON

As time moves on, we often change,
Yet we fail to see life's interchange.
We grow in ways we never planned,
But miss the bitterness at hand.

In youth, our hearts were soft and kind,
With love and joy, no hate to find.
But as we age, the world can scar,
And leave us angrier by far.

We fight for truths we hold so dear,
Yet we let our hearts be ruled by fear.
Our goodness, though sincere and strong,
Can hide where silent grudges throng.

To stand for right is just and true,
But love must guide us in all we do.
For what is gained if in our quest,
We let our hearts grow cold, no zest?

So look within, as years go by,
And keep your soul from growing dry.
For in the end, it's love that stays,
The light that guides us through our days.

GOD IS ALWAYS DOING 10,000 THINGS IN YOUR LIFE. YOU
MAY BE AWARE OF 3 OF THEM!

Wednesday, January 29, 2025

LOOK CLOSELY AT YOUR FACE TODAY

Look closely at your face today,
See what the years have brought your way.
Lay out the photos, young to old,
Watch how your story has been told.

From childhood's gaze, so pure and bright,
To youth's bold dreams and endless light.
But as the years have passed you by,
What shadows are now beneath your eyes?

As years went by, did joy depart?
Did bitterness creep into your heart?
The hardening you now may trace,
Is more than time upon your face.

Jealousy, and anger's hold,
Can etch the skin, can make it cold.
These lines are more than just of age,
They tell of life's more bitter page.

Reflect upon these changes deep,
The marks upon your face they keep.
Let go of what has made you hard,
Find peace within, let down your guard.

AGE MAKES YOU OLD ENOUGH TO KNOW BETTER. BUT
GOD MAKES YOU WISE ENOUGH TO DO BETTER!

Thursday, January 30, 2025

GOD'S LOVE EXTENDS TO EVERY SOUL

Health and wealth, they aren't the same,
Not equally given, not equally gained.
Flip a channel, and you will see,
A world of pain and poverty.

We watch the strong, the athletes' grace,
As millions suffer, their lives displaced.
But God's love reaches far and wide,
With special care for those denied.

The poor and weak, they touch God's heart,
But strength and beauty still have their part.
For God delights in talents shown,
In vibrant life, where hope has grown.

It's not a sin to be strong and bright,
To live in health, to feel the light.
God's love extends to every soul,
Each one a part, each one a whole.

Like a parent, God's love is true,
For every child, both old and new.
He smiles on those who brightly shine,
And holds the hurting, both divine.

IT IS NOT GREAT MEN AND WOMEN WHO CHANGE THE
WORLD, BUT WEAK MEN AND WOMEN IN THE HANDS OF
A GREAT GOD!

Friday, January 31, 2025

THE FIRE WITHIN US ALL

We all have struggles, dark and deep,
A fire within that doesn't sleep.
It's God's own image, wild and grand,
A force we struggle to understand.

Not just a spark, but a divine blaze,
That twists and turns in complex ways.
Inside us, fantasies run wild,
A shadowed side, both fierce and mild.

Daydreams we dare not share aloud,
Of glory, hate, and vengeance proud.
We hide them deep, out of sight,
Ashamed of thoughts that grip us tight.

But this wild fire is not our flaw,
It's part of us, natural and raw.
Our souls aren't sick, just misunderstood,
A shadowed depth that could be good.

So thank God for the struggles we face,
For in them, we find our truest grace.
In the wildness, there's a sacred glow,
A divine fire that helps us grow.

LIFE IS TOO SHORT AND ETERNITY IS TOO LONG TO LIVE
IT WITHOUT GOD!

WE FEAR THE JUDGEMENT

We fear the judgment that lays us bare,
Revealing secrets hidden there.
The darkest parts, we hide away,
Afraid of what the light might say.

We dread the thought of being seen,
Our faults exposed, our souls unclean.
Yet, we fear too, to be misread,
The truth inside left cold and dead.

The thought of judgment chills our bones,
A final day, where truth atones.
Yet deep within, we long to see,
Our full selves known, completely free.

For in that light, though flaws appear,
Our virtues too will shine as clear.
The darkness holds what we despise,
But light reveals where beauty lies.

Perhaps we sense, in judgment's fire,
A truth that lifts us ever higher.
For when we stand in God's pure sight,
We'll find both fear and peace unite.

DEAR GOD, IF TODAY I LOSE HOPE, PLEASE REMIND ME
THAT YOUR PLANS ARE BETTER THAN MY DREAMS!

THE PRESENTATION OF JESUS

Mary and Joseph, in joy and grace,
Took their child to the holy place.
To Jerusalem's temple, pure and bright,
Where Simeon saw the world's new light.

He held the child, and in his eye,
A revelation to the Gentiles did lie.
Anna too, with her watchful soul,
Found fulfillment, her heart made whole.

Their patience bore a lifetime's yield,
In this moment, a truth revealed.
Their waiting ended in joy profound,
For God's promise at last was found.

Patience calls us to see with care,
To be merciful, to love and share.
In our hearts, the Spirit waits,
Teaching a love that radiates.

In life and in our world today,
Do we judge, or pause and pray?
Patience offers grace and peace,
Through watchful hearts, all sarcasms cease.

THE CLOSER WE GET TO JESUS, THE SMALLER
EVERYTHING ELSE APPEARS!

GOD GIVES US TALENTS

God gives us talents, gifts so bright,
To use with love, to spread His light.
When we embrace what we've been given,
Our lives are blessed, our hearts are driven.

But if we let those gifts decay,
And never use them, come what may,
They turn to poison in our soul,
A bitter weight, a heavy toll.

Show me a person whose heart is cold,
Whose spirit's lost, whose dreams are old,
And there you'll find a soul in strife,
Unused gifts have marred his life.

A voice within us, soft yet clear,
Speaks to our talents, yearns to steer.
It calls us not to live in vain,
But use our gifts, to bear love's pain.

For we're not free to waste our days,
On selfish whims or fleeting praise.
Our lives must serve a greater call,
To give, to love, and thus stand tall.

I DID MY BEST AND GOD DID THE REST!

SOME SPIRITS SEEM TOO BRIGHT TO FADE

Sometimes it's hard to comprehend,
How a beloved one's life could ever end.
A vibrant pulse, a force so strong,
We cannot fathom it gone for long.

Some spirits seem too bright to fade,
Too full of love and light, so well-made.
How can such goodness cease to be?
How can their laughter fade to a memory?

Mary Magdalene at the tomb did cry,
For Jesus, she believed, had died.
Yet in her grief, she found Him near,
His spirit's presence, ever clear.

And so, the ones we love remain,
Their energy, not lost to pain.
It stays with us, it does not part,
Alive and pulsing in our heart.

To keep them close, we must believe,
Their spirit lives, though we may grieve.
In our every breath, in our every sigh,
Their love and life will never die.

WHEN THE SUNSHINE OF GOD'S LOVE MEETS THE
SHADOWS OF OUR SORROWS, THE RAINBOW OF HOPE
APPEARS!

Wednesday, February 5, 2025

WE MUST EMBRACE THE HUMAN RACE

The earth is round, its space is small,
We must unite, or surely fall.
In time, we meet, we share, we blend,
For borders break, and journeys end.

Resources thin, the land is tight,
We're bound to face this global plight.
As people move to find their place,
We must embrace the human race.

We too were once the strangers here,
With dreams of life and hopes unclear.
Now others come, with lives in tow,
To seek the same, to grow, to know.

What once was theirs, we took as ours,
Now tables turn with shifting powers.
It's our turn now to understand,
The fear of change within our land.

What goes around will come again,
A truth that echoes deep within.
So let us learn to share the space,
To build a world with open grace.

DEAR GOD, PLEASE HELP ME TODAY. GIVE ME STRENGTH
WHEN I AM WEAK, LEND ME A SHOULDER WHEN I NEED
TO CRY AND HELP ME UP WHEN I FALL!

Thursday, February 6, 2025

THE ILLUSION OF SUCCESS

Success is not just grit and might,
Nor failure, just a lack of fight.
We're not all born with an equal share,
Of chances, luck, or love and care.

Some start with riches, others none,
Some under clouds, others in sun.
Yet we believe that all can rise,
By merit, effort, in our eyes.

We praise the strong, call them the best,
And blame the weak for all the rest.
As if the paths we've walked were fair,
And every life had equal care.

We credit self for all we've done,
Forget the help, and the luck we've won.
And when we see the poor, the lost,
We blame them for the heavy cost.

So let us judge with kinder hearts,
For not all get the same head starts.
Success and failure, joy and pain,
Are shared by all in life's great game.

THE SMILE ON MY FACE DOESN'T MEAN MY LIFE IS
PERECT. I JUST APPRECIATE WHAT I HAVE AND HOW GOD
HAS BLESSED ME.

GOD'S LOVE NEVER GOES AWAY

Jesus taught a better way,
A path of love for every day.
The Sermon's words, so pure and clear,
Could change the world if we could hear.

Yet self-interest clouds our sight,
Resisting what is just and right.
His teachings weren't what conquered sin,
But His death, where love did win.

No power, no force, no grand display,
Just a grain of wheat in humble clay.
Through His dying, truth took root,
And in the end, it bore great fruit.

He didn't use persuasive might,
Or dazzle with some blinding light.
He held to love through every breath,
Even as He faced His own death.

The powers thought they'd have their say,
But God's love never goes away.
By raising Jesus from the grave,
God showed the world what truth can save.

MORE JESUS, LESS DRAMA. LESS SELFISHNESS. LESS
COMPLAINING. LESS BITTERNESS. LESS GOSSIP. LESS ME.
MORE JESUS!

Saturday, February 8, 2025

WE SEARCH FOR GOD IN MANY WAYS

We search for God in many ways,
Unknowing, through our busy days.
We think it's through a prayer or hymn,
But often it's in life's own rhythm.

In seeking joy, we chase the light,
In love and pleasure, day and night.
We think we're seeking just our bliss,
But God is what we truly miss.

We strive for meaning, crave a touch,
A deeper truth, we want so much.
In every heartbeat, every sigh,
We seek the One beyond the sky.

Our souls are restless, filled with fire,
An endless quest, a deep desire.
We dive into the world's embrace,
Unknowing it's God's love we chase.

Through earthly quests and lofty dreams,
In every search, God's presence beams.
For in our hearts, divine flames burn,
And all our paths to Him return.

LORD, HELP ME TO LOVE LIKE I HAVE BEEN LOVED!

Sunday, February 9, 2025

JESUS' WORDS WELCOME ALL

The apostles, with good intent,
Would guard the path where Jesus went.
They'd turn away the lost, the small,
But Jesus' words would welcome all.

"Let them come!" He'd softly say,
To those the world would push away.
The children, sinners, all the same,
He welcomed each, He knew their name.

Even now, we try to shield,
God's mercy from those in the field.
We judge who's worthy, who's not right,
But Jesus calls them to the light.

No need to guard God's endless grace,
For every soul can find a place.
Regardless of their life's own tale,
In God's embrace, they cannot fail.

So let them come, the weak, the lost,
For Jesus bore the highest cost.
He wants them all, no one denied,
Inviting all to come inside.

JESUS THOUGHT YOU WERE WORTH LEAVING HEAVEN FOR!

FROM ONE WOMB INTO ANOTHER

We are born from one womb, safe and warm,
Into another, as our life takes form.
A second womb, the world so wide,
Where we grow, where we reside.

This world, a womb that gives us care,
Provides us light and ample air.
It nurtures us through each long day,
And gives us hope along the way.

When young and strong, we feel secure,
No need for light as we mature.
It's vast and bright compared to before,
Yet still a womb, with so much more.

In this warm space, we grow and thrive,
In this secure place, we feel alive.
But as we age, a question stirs,
Is there more light than what occurs?

Left to ourselves, we cannot tell,
If beyond this womb lies heaven or hell.
Yet deep within, a faint light gleams,
Whispering to us of greater dreams.

GOD GAVE US EYES TO SEE THE BEAUTY IN NATURE AND
HEARTS TO SEE THE BEAUTY IN EACH OTHER!

GOD'S MERCY IS A BOUNDLESS SEA

We cannot make God turn away,
His love for us will never sway.
No act of ours can spark His ire,
For God is love, our heart's desire.

But we, ourselves, can feel the sting,
Of guilt and shame that our actions bring.
It's not God's wrath that haunts our soul,
But self-reproach that takes its toll.

No sin can make God hate our name,
Yet we can drown in self-placed blame.
Forgiveness from God flows like a stream,
But self-forgiveness can seem like a dream.

God's mercy is a boundless sea,
Yet we, ourselves, can fail to see,
That love and grace are ever near,
While we hold on to guilt and fear.

The problem's not with God above,
Who meets our faults with endless love.
It's in our hearts where struggles brew,
To see ourselves as God sees us, ever new.

WHEN YOU'RE TEMPTED TO LOSE PATIENCE WITH
SOMEONE, THINK HOW PATIENT GOD HAS BEEN WITH
YOU!

Wednesday, February 12, 2025

Lincoln's Birthday

THINK OF LINCOLN

Think of Lincoln, the words they said,
The calumnies and criticisms they spread.
Caricatures drawn with unjust might,
Yet today, we see his light.

With insight clear, he wrote with grace,
Ignoring attacks, he kept his pace.
"If I read them all," he wisely knew,
"No other business I could pursue."

"I'll do my best, until the end,"
His steadfast resolve, a truthful friend.
"If the end is right, words won't prevail,
If wrong, even angels' praise will fail."

Critics may carp, and voices may jeer,
But truth and justice persevere.
Lincoln's style, now praised and bright,
Shines through history, a guiding light.

So let us learn from his noble stand,
To do our best, with heart and hand.
For in the end, it's deeds that last,
Through trials faced, our legacy cast.

THE THINGS YOU TAKE FOR GRANTED, SOMEONE ELSE IS
PRAYING FOR!

ONE ADDICTION WE APPLAUD

There's one addiction we applaud,
To overwork, we give a nod.
While others seek a cure for pain,
We see in work a worthy gain.

We wear our busyness like a shield,
To cover wounds that never healed.
Too many tasks, too short a time,
Our frantic pace becomes a climb.

I recognize the symptoms now,
The endless rush, the furrowed brow.
The clock's a foe we can't outrun,
No time to see the rising sun.

But why this rush, this frantic pace?
What drives us in this endless race?
It's loneliness we try to hide,
In work's embrace, we set it aside.

So pause, take time, let stillness grow,
And feel the life you barely know.
For in the quiet, love can thrive,
And loneliness will not survive.

THE WORLD SEES ONLY WHAT YOU DO. GOD SEES WHY
YOU DO IT!

Friday, February 14, 2025

Valentine's Day

ON THIS VALENTINE'S DAY

Dear Jesus, on this Valentine's Day, I bring,
A hopeful heart that dares to sing.
A heart sometimes broken, yet it beats with grace,
For in every piece, it's Your love I trace.

A heart that's grateful, a heart that's torn,
A heart that's weary, yet newly born.
Through disappointment and silent cries,
You see the beauty and no disguise.

A heart that struggles, that longs for peace,
A heart that finds in You its release.
You weave through minefields with gentle care,
To heal the wounds I often bear.

In broken hearts, Your power shines,
A testimony to Your love's designs.
In every crack, Your light does gleam,
My resurrected, hopeful dream.

For even in the shattered parts,
There lies the beauty for all brave hearts.
You redeemed the world with Your great love,
So my heart's become a gift from above

GOD'S LOVE SUPPY IS NEVER EMPTY!

THERE'S NEVER ENOUGH TIME

There's never enough time in the day,
So much to do, so much to say.
Our lives are like bags packed too tight,
Bursting with tasks from morning to night.

We feel the clock is running fast,
Each second gone, forever past.
Unfinished tasks weigh on our mind,
So much to do, no space left to find.

A constant rush, we're always late,
Chasing a list that will never abate.
There's always something left behind,
A nagging thought within the mind.

But time's not flawed, it's we who strive,
To do so much more than just survive.
God gave us time, enough for all,
To live with grace, to heed the call.

It's not time's fault we feel this way,
But it's our own desire to overplay.
We crave to do more behind life's plough,
Forgetting to breathe, to live in the now.

WHEN GOD SEES YOU DOING YOUR PART, DEVELOPING
WHAT GOD HAS GIVEN YOU, THEN GOD WILL OPEN
DOORS THAT NO ONE CAN SHUT!

JESUS WALKED THE EARTH UNARMED

Jesus walked the earth unarmed,
A peaceful soul who caused alarm.
The powers feared his gentle way,
More than a killer on display.

Barabbas, armed and full of hate,
Was less a threat to their estate.
"Release for us this violent man,"
But not the one with a peaceful plan.

They sensed in Jesus a deeper threat,
In non-violence, a danger set.
To turn the cheek, to love, forgive,
Was more than they could let him live.

Jesus' moral truth, His peaceful way,
Shook the foundations of their day.
Disarmed and dangerous, He stood tall,
A threat that could unseat them all.

For disarmed souls with hearts of light,
Expose the wrong, confront the night.
With no weapon but integrity,
They challenge all that ought not to be.

MIRROR, MIRROR ON THE WALL, DO YOU SEE CHRIST IN
ME AT ALL?

WE FOUGHT THE CALL TO BED

As children, we fought the call to bed,
Though tired eyes and heavy head.
We didn't want to leave the fun,
While life was buzzing, and far from done.

The lights still bright, the voices cheer,
We feared the joy we wouldn't hear.
Exhausted, yet we stayed awake,
Afraid of all we'd have to forsake.

That fear remains as we grow old,
The same reluctance, firm and bold.
To leave the world after so many years,
Is one of death's most haunting fears.

We dread the thought of missing more,
Of walking through that final door.
To be taken from the vibrant scene,
While life continues on every screen.

But even when we're called away,
Life moves on in its own way.
Though hard to leave, we must concede,
The party on earth is not for us to lead.

PEOPLE MAY NOT THANK YOU. YOU MAY NOT GET THE
CREDIT YOU DESERVE. NOBODY MAY GIVE YOU
APPLAUSE. BUT WHEN YOU SERVE OTHERS, THERE IS
APPLAUSE FOR YOU IN HEAVEN!

Tuesday, February 18, 2025

WE ONCE STILL HELD TO WHAT WAS RIGHT

When did we lose the simple art,
Of treating others with a kind heart?
Though we may disagree or fight,
We once still held to what was right.

Respect and courtesy fade away,
Replaced by harshness in what we say.
From leaders down to an online spat,
Basic decency seems to fall flat.

Honesty and manners seem now rare,
With no accountability or care.
What once was wrong, we now defend,
As if true kindness was just a pretend.

The things we taught to children young,
To hold their tongues when words were flung,
Are now dismissed as weakness, plain,
While cruelty, it seems, must ever reign.

Civility, once held so high,
Has faded as we let it die.
But we must mourn and seek to mend,
A world where kindness should never end.

GOD, HELP ME TO RESPOND WITH LOVE BEFORE I REACT
WITH ANGER!

AT THAT TABLE ALL WILL SHARE

God's call is clear, more strong today,
To show respect in every way.
For we must dine in heaven's grace,
And share one table, face to face.

Though here on earth we may contend,
With those we see as foe, not friend,
We cannot claim that heavenly seat,
By hatred's power or forceful feat.

For at that table, all will share,
The love and kindness seated there.
And though we differ here on earth,
In heaven, we will know our worth.

Not everyone we meet will find,
A place within our heart or mind.
But at God's feast, both great and small,
Will treat each other best of all.

So let us learn while still we live,
To show respect, to love, forgive.
For at that table, we will see,
The grace of perfect unity.

TODAY WILL NEVER COME AGAIN! BE A BLESSING! BE A
FRIEND! ENCOURAGE SOMEONE! TAKE TIME TO CARE!
LET YOUR WORDS HEAL AND NOT WOUND!

Thursday, February 20, 2025

WE BRING AN ENERGY

We bring an energy, unseen but true,
That colors the room in shades of hue.
When we walk in, the air will change,
Our spirit leaves a lasting range.

If we bring joy, concern, and grace,
A warmth will settle in that space.
That kindness lingers, soft and bright,
Even well into the darkest night.

But if we carry anger's fire,
Or jealousy and dark desire,
That tension stays when we are gone,
A shadow cast, still lingering on.

The spirit left when we depart,
Remains within each mind and heart.
The tone we set will ripple wide,
A hidden force we cannot hide.

So may we strive to leave behind,
A presence warm, sincere, and kind.
For what we give in every way,
Will live in hearts beyond our stay.

IF THERE'S A GOLIATH IN FRONT OF YOU, THAT MEANS
THERE IS A DAVID INSIDE OF YOU!

Friday, February 21, 2025

NO ONE'S AN ISLAND, TRULY ALONE

No one's an island, truly alone,
Our private acts are widely known.
For what we do in silent space,
Will ripple out, become a quiet trace.

Each thought we think, though kept inside,
Can touch the world, though we may hide.
Our hearts connect in ways unseen,
In light or dark, or in between.

Jesus taught, and we must heed,
It's not just actions, but thoughts we breed.
To think with hate is still to harm,
For even thoughts can raise an alarm.

We sense it deep, in hearts that know,
Our private deeds help others grow.
Or hurt them too, when left unkind,
For nothing's truly kept confined.

So let us tend our inner place,
With love and light, and gentle grace.
For every thought, though none may see,
Affects the world, affects the "we."

IF GOD IS MAKING YOU WAIT, THEN BE PREPARED TO
RECEIVE MORE THAN WHAT YOU ASKED FOR!

Saturday, February 22, 2025

WE SEEK A SOUL TO UNDERSTAND

Moral loneliness, a deep, soft ache,
For someone who knows what's at stake.
We seek a soul to understand,
To touch our heart, to hold our hand.

We're restless beings, never still,
Despite the love we sometimes feel.
A longing haunts us, undefined,
A home we search for, so hard to find.

We're not at peace, but always yearn,
For love's pure light, for which we burn.
Rest comes in glimpses, brief and sweet,
But full satisfaction we seldom meet.

Before we were born, God's kiss was placed,
Upon our souls, never to be erased.
We seek that kiss in all we do,
Measuring life by what we once knew.

For what we want, beyond our skin,
Is someone who will see within.
A soul who honors all we are,
The one we seek, both near and far.

THERE ISN'T ENOUGH ROOM IN YOUR MIND FOR BOTH
WORRY AND FAITH. YOU MUST DECIDE WHICH ONE WILL
LIVE THERE!

Sunday, February 23, 2025

COMPASSION IS MORE THAN A KIND EMBRACE

Compassion is more than a kind embrace,
It's building a world with love and grace.
Strategies and structures to lift the low,
For those who suffer, our care must show.

When systems fail and cracks appear,
It's up to us to act and persevere.
Loved into action by God's own hand,
We challenge the order, we take a stand.

To change the plight of the marginalized,
We must rise up, with justice realized.
To fail this call is to lose the light,
Of God within our society's fight.

Compassionate hearts must lead the way,
To find solutions, to pave the way.
In love and action, our faith is found,
In lifting others, up on solid ground.

So let us work with purpose and might,
To build a world where all is right.
In unity, we rise above the fray,
With God's compassion lighting the way.

WHEN YOU LOVE YOUR ENEMIES, YOU REVEAL WHAT
KIND OF GOD YOUR GOD IS!

Monday, February 24, 2025

LET VIOLENCE CEASE

God, let violence cease, please end the fight,
No more bloodshed, bring peace tonight.
Your heart breaks for the lost and left behind,
Orphaned children, families in need, the confined.

We pray for peace, let conflict cease,
Bring your reconciliation, a world at ease.
Give wisdom to leaders, discernment to guide,
Let love and justice worldwide abide.

Help us to be bold, advocates of peace,
In our communities, let hope increase.
Agents of change, with courage to stand,
For a future of harmony in every land.

God, grant us strength to heal and mend,
To lift up the fallen, on you we depend.
In your love, we find our grace,
Uniting the world in your embrace.

Let our hearts be open, our spirits free,
To work for peace and unity.
For in your light, we find our way,
Bringing hope to each new day.

ONE GOOD REASON TO PRAY – GOD CAN DO MORE IN A
SECOND THAN YOU CAN DO FOR YOURSELF IN A
LIFETIME!

THE GOOD YOU SEEK

The good you seek won't come from things,
Not from jewels or the wealth they bring.
For material goods are mere displays,
Of ideas of good in countless ways.

The true treasures in life, they never fade,
Invisible, eternal, lovingly made.
They don't break or go out of style,
But last forever, mile after mile.

A loving thought, a creative spark,
These are the joys that light the dark.
They fill the heart with endless cheer,
Their value grows, year after year.

So cherish the thoughts that lift your soul,
For they are the things that make you whole.
Enjoy the love and ideas you share,
For they are treasures beyond compare.

Embrace the good that's deep within,
The light of life that will never dim.
For in these moments, you will find,
The real good things that free your mind.

HAVE YOU PRAYED ABOUT IT AS MUCH AS YOU HAVE
TALKED ABOUT IT?

EYES THAT GLANCE

Some go through life with eyes that glance,
Seeing the surface, yet missing the dance.
They look at the image, but not the core,
Vision is present, but perception is poor.

In a painting, they see colors bold,
But miss the genius the brushstrokes hold.
On a journey, they walk the road,
Yet miss the beauty of the vast abode.

In meals, they eat, their hunger sated,
But miss the beauty that's understated.
The china's charm, the wine's embrace,
The subtle joys that life can trace.

If life were a poem, they'd read each line,
But miss the passion, of the poet's design.
Without insight, life fades away,
Into a dull routine, a lifeless play.

So open your eyes, embrace each hue,
See the depth, the essence, the view.
Perceive the world with a mindful heart,
And find the magic that sets your life apart.

SOMETIMES I JUST LOOK UP, SMILE AND SAY, "I KNOW
THAT WAS YOU!" THANK YOU GOD!

A SURGEON IN A BUSY PLACE

A well-known surgeon in a busy place,
Would always seek a moment of grace.
Alone he stood before each task,
In silence, he would quietly ask.

A young doctor asked with curiosity,
If these moments held a special key.
The surgeon nodded, calm and wise,
And shared the truth behind his eyes.

"Before each operation, I pray,
For guidance to see me through the day.
The Great Physician's hand I seek,
To guide me when my skills feel weak."

"There were times I didn't know what to do,
But then came a power, strong and true.
A strength from God to carry on,
In His presence, my doubts were gone."

"I wouldn't dare to start my work alone,
Without first seeking His guiding tone.
So in every operation, His light I seek,
For in God's strength, I am not weak."

I WISH I COULD GIVE GOD A HUG FOR ALL GOD HAS
DONE FOR ME!

Friday, February 28, 2025

SOMETIMES WE FORGET

Sometimes we forget, but it's still true,
Not long ago, we were children too.
With faith unwavering, joy in their play,
Children find miracles in every day.

As adults, our view often shifts away,
But wonder and magic still have a say.
Attitudes change, but the world remains,
Full of miracles and wondrous gains.

Miracles occur when someone cares,
When kindness is shown, and love repairs.
Animosity fades with a compassionate hand,
Simple acts of love, are miracles so grand.

In a world where cynicism seems to reign,
"Anything is possible" can ease the pain.
With hope in our hearts, we can create,
Miracles in life, since it's never too late.

So next time you need a miracle's glow,
Remember, it's within you to bestow.
With love and care, you hold the key,
To create miracles, for all to see.

WHEN YOU LET GO, SOMETHING MAGICAL HAPPENS.
YOU GIVE GOD ROOM TO WORK!

Saturday, March 1, 2025

LIFE'S TRADE-OFFS

Life is filled with choices, trade-offs we make,
Sacrifices given, for the paths we take.
In marriage and work, in the children we raise,
At every turn, we choose our ways.

We give up some freedoms, for others we gain,
With each chosen path, there's joy and pain.
The scenic roads missed, left in the past,
For the one we travel, hopes are cast.

In each decision, a price is paid,
In dreams pursued, and dreams delayed.
We believe in worth, in what we choose,
Hoping the gains outweigh what we lose.

Every journey made, a different view,
Sacrifices taken, for something new.
Believing in value, greater than before,
That the cost is worth, what we adore.

In life's trade-offs, we find our place,
Seeking meaning, in every space.
For every sacrifice, there's something we gain,
In the balance of life, both joy and pain.

STOP FOCUSING ON HOW STRESSED YOU ARE AND
REMEMBER HOW BLESSED YOU ARE!

Sunday, March 2, 2025

INTEREST AND COMMITMENT

There's a difference, clear and bright,
Between interest and commitment's light.
Interest acts when it's easy to see,
But commitment stands firm, no matter the plea.

When you're interested, it's when you please,
But commitment makes no room for ease.
Excuses fade, determination thrives,
In commitment, true service survives.

To serve Christ with all that we can,
Takes sacrifice, it's part of the plan.
Willing to give, to see His will done,
In the kingdom of God, we all are one.

Bearing fruit that lasts, not fades,
Through our work, the foundation is laid.
Witness and labor, with hearts so pure,
In Christ's love, we find our cure.

So be committed, in every way,
In Christ's service, come what may.
With no excuses, let's bear the load,
Together, we walk the righteous road.

JESUS CAN TURN WATER INTO WINE, BUT JESUS CAN'T
TURN WHINING INTO ANYTHING!

Monday, March 3, 2025

WHEN FAITH IS JUST A PART

When faith is just a part, not the whole,
You miss the essence, the life of the soul.
Stopping by to pay your dues,
Isn't enough if it's God you choose.

If you squeeze God into your busy day,
But value more the worldly way,
You show yourself in a lesser light,
An impostor in the grandest sight.

Faith should be the vibrant core,
The guiding light that we adore.
Not just a task or fleeting thought,
But the center where true life is sought.

Without the festive garment worn,
You stand at the feast, forlorn.
Realize the kingdom's joyous call,
Where God has prepared the best for all.

So let your faith be bold and bright,
Not squeezed between the day and night.
Make it the heart of all you do,
And life will be vibrant, deep, and true.

IF YOU SAW THE SIZE OF THE BLESSING COMING YOUR
WAY, YOU WOULD UNDERSTAND THE MAGNITUDE OF
THE BATTLE YOU ARE FIGHTING!

Tuesday, March 4, 2025

START EACH DAY

Each morning brings a rush of dreams,
Like wild animals coming in streams.
But in the quiet, we must find,
A voice of peace to still the mind.

Before the chaos takes its hold,
Embrace the life that's calm and bold.
Let go of fears, and gently rest,
In God's embrace, forever blessed.

To yield to God, we must be free,
From every worldly vanity.
In silence, find the strength to rise,
Empowered by the Lord's supplies.

For only when we're still and clear,
Can God's true power draw us near.
Through us, His love and light can shine,
To heal the world with grace divine.

So start each day with an open heart,
And let the Spirit play its part.
For in this yielding, we become,
The vessels of His kingdom come

TODAY DO THE THINGS THAT FEED YOUR SOUL AND NOT
YOUR EGO AND YOU'LL BE HAPPY!

Wednesday, March 5, 2025

Ash Wednesday

THE CHURCH PUTS ASHES ON OUR BROW

The church puts ashes on our brow,
A mark of time to pause for now.
In Lent, we sit among the dust,
Reflecting on what broke our trust.

We grieve the things we've done in haste,
The times we strayed, the love we waste.
We stop the rush, the frantic pace,
To let the ashes find their place.

For Lent is not a time to strive,
But for quiet growth to come alive.
The ashes work in ways unknown,
In stillness, seeds of grace are sown.

We need not grasp their purpose well,
For ashes hold a patient spell.
They've watched us stumble, fall, and rise,
Through every season, truth applies.

So sit with them, as seasons turn,
In humble silence, let them burn.
For Lent's a time to wait and see,
The silent work of mystery.

IF YOU SPEND YOUR TIME PRAYING FOR PEOPLE
INSTEAD OF TALKING ABOUT THEM, YOU'LL GET BETTER
RESULTS!

Thursday, March 6, 2025

ASHES FELT SO TRUE

On Ash Wednesday, the ashes felt so true,
Reflecting dreams burned down, life's residue.
Certain hopes, innocence, and youthful might,
Now lay in ashes, not lost from sight.

A sense of power, goodness once I knew,
Reduced to dust, like morning dew.
I took the ashes, with no rush to clean,
Nor thrill to leave them, a silent sheen.

For years these ashes, patient and kind,
Challenged my soul, yet peace did find.
Accepting my reactions, like God's own grace,
They spoke of demons I had to face.

This year, the cross on my forehead stayed,
Belonging there, where my fears played.
Ashes marking, a symbol profound,
Of struggles and growth, where truths are found.

Through Lent, these ashes, my silent guide,
Revealed the battles within I cannot hide.
Accepting, challenging, in their embrace,
Leading me to confront, and find God's grace.

IT'S CRAZY HOW GOD FORGIVES US DAILY, YET WE
HOLD GRUDGES FOREVER!

GIVE UP FOR LENT

Give up grumbling, give thanks instead,
Let gratitude fill your heart and head.
Constructive words can help you grow,
But moaning dims the brightest glow.

Give up ten minutes in your bed,
Spend that time in prayer instead.
A moment's prayer can shape your day,
Keep focused, let God guide your way.

Give up picking at faults alone,
See the best in others shown.
Overlook faults and you will find,
That grace returns in kindred kind.

Give up the unkind words you say,
Speak with love in every way.
A smile or kind deed's cost is small,
But lifts the hearts of one and all.

Give up worries, such a heavy load,
Trust in God as you travel your road.
Anxiety steals your peace and rest,
In God's grace, you are truly blessed.

WHATEVER YOUR PROBLEM, DO NOT NURSE IT, CURSE
IT, OR REHEARSE IT. JUST TURN IT OVER TO GOD AND
LET GOD REVERSE IT.

Saturday, March 8, 2025

LOW BATTERY

One day while typing, my screen went black,
A warning flashed to bring me back.
"Low battery," it did declare,
A call for spiritual repair.

Like devices, we need to recharge too,
Our souls need power to renew.
To reflect Jesus, bright and clear,
We must in prayer, draw Him near.

To be like Him in all we do,
We need His presence to imbue.
Reflect on Him, His words of grace,
To find in prayer our sacred place.

There's wisdom in this simple phrase,
Reflect on Jesus all our days.
For in His love, we find our might,
To shine His light in the darkest night.

So each morning, take the time,
Reflect on the parables, on truths sublime.
In Lent, let Jesus be your guide,
With Him in your heart, walk by His side.

GOD'S LOVE CAN'T BE EXPLAINED, ONLY EXPERIENCED!

Sunday, March 9, 2025

FORTY DAYS OF LENT

Jesus wandered for forty days,
In the wilderness, in silent praise.
A time to pause, reflect, and pray,
Preparing our hearts for Easter Day.

In hurried lives, let's not rush by,
These sacred days beneath the sky.
We count down birthdays and holidays,
But Lent's a gift, not just a phase.

Let's not waste time in anxious wait,
With Easter's coming joy, let's cultivate.
A deeper dive into our soul,
To seek and find a heart made whole.

See Jesus walk the human path,
His choices, struggles, and the aftermath.
His journey mirrors our own fight,
To choose what's good, true and right.

This Lent, may we find strength anew,
In quiet moments, in skies of blue.
Let God remaking us fill our core,
Transforming us forevermore.

THE LOVE OF JESUS IS THE LOVE YOU AND I HAVE BEEN
LOOKING FOR ALL OUR LIVES!

Monday, March 10, 2025

JUSTICE MUST PRECEDE TRUE PEACE

Our way of life is built on greed,
A thirst for more, an endless need.
We live believing that all we gain,
By right is ours, without disdain.

Excess is praised, success defined,
By what we own, by what's left behind.
Our culture feeds this cancer's spread,
As others starve, we're overfed.

We strive to take all life can give,
No thought for those who barely live.
Their struggles mean so little here,
Our wealth amassed, their futures unclear.

Then once we have what we desire,
We seek for peace, we douse the fire.
Enraged if others dare to claim,
A share of what we proudly name.

But justice must precede true peace,
Without it, conflicts never cease.
The poor's cry is unheard, their voices dim,
Sometimes in terror, they find their hymn.

TO HEAR GOD'S VOICE IN YOU, YOU MUST TURN DOWN
THE WORLD'S VOLUME!

MEASURING OUR WORTH

God's love does not compare or rank,
In His embrace, no child is a blank.
But in this world, we often see,
A constant need for rivalry.

Intelligence and beauty judged,
Success and failure, the lines are smudged.
We think love follows in this vein,
And we find ourselves in a constant strain.

When others earn their praise and fame,
We question why we're not the same.
Awards and trophies that others gain,
Can stir in us a quiet pain.

We're taught to measure our worth,
In grades and scores, from our birth.
We chase these marks, but joy is lost,
In life's great race, at what a cost.

Yet God's own love does not compare,
In His eyes, all fully merit His care.
Though hard to grasp and hard to see,
His love is always there for you and me.

GOD IS BIGGER THAN – YOUR PAST, DEPRESSION, PAIN,
HATE, ANGER, DOUBT, FEAR, SHAME, ANXIETY,
LONELINESS, SCARS, AND THIS WORLD!

Wednesday, March 12, 2025

LOVE IS TAKING A RISK

Love is all about taking a risk,
But not all risks are founded on bliss.
Falling in love's like falling from a height,
An abandonment into the unknown night.

It's a letting go, a release of brakes,
Exposing the heart to both joys and aches.
We lay ourselves bare to hurt and heal,
Vulnerable to what we might feel.

Letting another into our core,
To touch our spirit, our heart, and more.
A powerful and threatening dance,
Love's embrace, is a risky chance.

Love carries the fire of God's own grace,
Healing wounds in a sacred space.
Filling voids, giving life new meaning,
Or leaving scars that keep us reeling.

Risk loving, but measure it right,
Will it bring God's spirit, or endless night?
In love's embrace, seek the divine,
Let it be a path to where hearts align.

THE KEYS TO LIFE: 1. GOD FIRST, 2. LOVE ONE ANOTHER,
3. NEVER HATE, 4. GIVE GENEROUSLY, 5. LIVE SIMPLY,
6. FORGIVE QUICKLY, 7. BE KIND ALWAYS!

Thursday, March 13, 2025

GOD'S GRACE SHINES THROUGH

Where God's grace shines through,
We help another, in all that we do.
Feeding hearts and spirits in need,
In simple acts, we plant love's seed.

Instead of a ball game, time we give,
To a lonely soul, to help them live.
In nursing homes, where families are rare,
We share our love, we show we care.

Instead of coffee and our morning read,
We teach Sunday school, and plant a faith seed.
Dressed and ready, we share our time,
In teaching love, and lessons divine.

Instead of games on screens so bright,
We listen to friends through day and night.
Though tired and burdened, we lend an ear,
Despite their struggles, we stay ever near.

These acts may seem small, miracles few,
But they bring meaning, in all we do.
God's grace in us, in every part,
Bringing significance, filling the heart.

GOOD PEOPLE ARE LIKE CANDLES.....THEY BURN
THEMSELVES UP TO GIVE LIGHT TO OTHERS!

A BIKE RIDE

Learning to ride, a moment so bold,
When the hands that held you, let go their hold.
Maybe you crashed, and had to start anew,
But then you soared, with the sky so blue.

"Hey, Mom, look at me!" you cried with glee,
Zooming around, feeling so free.
The breeze in your face, the joy in your heart,
In that moment, you felt alive, a work of art.

That joy so full, your heart did pound,
In that brief second, freedom you found.
The cost was worth it, every fall and scrape,
For the thrill of the ride, the joy did shape.

Such moments are parables, for us to see,
How God upholds, how faith sets us free.
Assuming the cost, we travel by faith,
In His hands, we find joy, a straighter path.

The Christian finds, in trials and grace,
That exhilarating joy, in God's embrace.
With each step of faith, each brave endeavor,
We ride with God, both now and forever.

THE WILL OF GOD WILL NEVER TAKE YOU WHERE THE
GRACE OF GOD WILL NOT PROTECT YOU!

WHEN WE WAIT

When we wait, we face the truth inside,
Some things are beyond our control and pride.
We love to think we shape our fate,
Masters of destiny, and never late.

Hard work can take us far, it's true,
With focus and prep, so much we can do.
But some things take their own sweet time,
Not all can be hurried or fit to rhyme.

Recuperation needs patience and care,
Grief takes time, a burden to bear.
A young heart learns what it means to be free,
Responsibility blooms, but not instantly.

In life, two realities stand side by side,
Some things you earn, and some you bide.
Waiting is hard, patience is rare,
Yet some things take time to prepare.

Though we wish to rush and hasten fate,
There's wisdom found when we choose to wait.
In every pause, we find life's gentle flow,
There's growth and grace as we come to know.

EVEN IF LIFE GIVES YOU 1,000 REASONS TO QUIT, GOD
WILL GIVE YOU 1,001 REASONS TO KEEP GOING!

Sunday, March 16, 2025

YOUR EYE ON JESUS

Keep your eye on Jesus, let Him lead the way,
Through life's distractions, don't be led astray.
The world's allure and its fleeting charms,
Can't compare to the safety of His arms.

Don't be swayed by politics or peer pressure's call,
Or a culture that says your faith is too small.
Stay firm and true to your guiding light,
In the face of doubt, hold Jesus tight.

Keeping your eye on Jesus doesn't mean,
That you disengage from the worldly scene.
But align your heart and your mind each day,
With His teachings guiding your way.

Priorities set straight, perspective clear,
With God as your compass, you'll have no fear.
Engage with the world, but keep in mind,
In Jesus' love, true strength you'll find.

So let Him be your anchor, your guide and friend,
In every decision, on Him you can depend.
Keep your eye on Jesus, through storm and strife,
For in Him, you'll find the purpose of life.

GOD DOESN'T GIVE US WHAT WE CAN HANDLE. GOD
HELPS US HANDLE WHAT WE ARE GIVEN.

Monday, March 17, 2025

St. Patrick's Day

ST. PATRICK SPOKE OF LOVE AND PEACE

St. Patrick came upon two kin,
Their quarrel loud, their patience thin.
They fought for land, their father's share,
And neither brother seemed to care.

With words of anger, fists took flight,
St. Patrick feared a deadly fight.
One raised a rock with deadly aim,
Patrick prayed, to halt the blame.

In that moment, both froze like stone,
Their bodies stiff, their anger shown.
They saw the world but couldn't act,
A lesson taught with heaven's pact.

St. Patrick spoke of love and peace,
Of how their fight should truly cease.
When turned to men, they stood amazed,
Their hearts transformed, their anger razed.

From that day forth, they stood as one,
Their battles past, their hatred done.
For Patrick's prayer had set them free,
To live in love and unity.

BROKEN THINGS CAN BECOME BLESSINGS IF YOU LET
GOD DO THE MENDING!

Tuesday, March 18, 2025

GIVE THANKS

I take the good things and give thanks to the skies,
For blessings received, and joys that arise.
I examine the bad, the feelings they bring,
To learn and grow, to understand everything.

Inside me, I look at what I feel,
Not just thoughts, but emotions real.
"What did I feel?" I ask each day,
To understand what my heart has to say.

Feelings are guides, they hold a key,
To unlock the truths inside of me.
Not to control, but to comprehend,
The messages they silently send.

To master my feelings, not rule with might,
But to see them clearly, in a gentle light.
Each emotion has a tale to tell,
Of lessons learned, and ways to excel.

In knowing myself, I find my way,
With God's guidance, I pray each day.
To be in tune with my heart's refrain,
And live a life of growth and gain.

WHERE THERE IS HOPE, THERE IS FAITH. WHERE THERE
IS FAITH, MIRACLES DO HAPPEN!

Wednesday, March 19, 2025

St. Joseph's Day

ST. JOSEPH SPOKE NO WORDS

St. Joseph spoke no words, it's true,
But trusted God in all he'd do.
In silence, strength was quietly sown,
His actions spoke where none were known.

Sometimes in life, we feel unseen,
Our dreams, once bright, no longer gleam.
We think we've been forgotten here,
Our worth dismissed, our hearts unclear.

Yet Joseph's path can help us see,
That silent strength brings victory.
In supporting others, we find our role,
In helping them, we make life whole.

Not every life is praised by name,
But some in silence rise to fame.
In steadfast faith, in gentle care,
We find our place in God's great prayer.

So let us live, in Joseph's way,
With patience, love, and truth each day.
For quiet hearts, both pure and kind,
Leave lasting legacies behind.

YOU'RE A GOD WHO HAS EVERYTHING…..AND STILL
YOU WANT ME!

Thursday, March 20, 2025

"DO NOT BE AFRAID"

"Do not be afraid," the angels proclaim,
Words of comfort, are always the same.
To Abraham and Moses, courage they lend,
To Mary and Joseph, it's faith they send.

Shepherds in the fields hear this refrain,
Paul in his cell finds strength in the chain.
Women at Easter, come seeking the Lord,
To disciples in storms, fear is ignored.

Humans are fearful, it's often said,
We need faith to guide us, where angels tread.
In moments of doubt and times of despair,
"Do not be afraid" is a call to prayer.

Faith is the anchor in life's stormy seas,
A light in the darkness, a gentle breeze.
For courage and strength, we look above,
Finding solace in God's unending love.

So when fear rises and shadows creep,
Remember these words, in your heart they'll keep.
With faith as your guide, hold steady and true,
"Do not be afraid," for God is with you.

MAKE YOUR PRAYERS BIGGER THAN YOUR FEARS!

TRUE LISTENING

A mother took her boy, aged ten,
To see the doctor once again.
His hearing seemed to have a flaw,
She needed to know what the doctor saw.

The doctor examined, long and deep,
And on the boy's shoulder, his hand did keep.
"Do you have trouble hearing, my son?"
"I hear just fine, but I listen to none."

If we have the Spirit, our hearts will open wide,
We'll hear truth, with understanding as our guide.
Not just the sounds, but the meaning profound,
In the whispers of faith, where wisdom is found.

To listen well is a gift so rare,
To truly hear, and deeply care.
For in those moments, we find our way,
To understand and not just say.

So let's be mindful, in what we seek,
To hear with hearts, humble and meek.
For in the Spirit, we'll find our part,
Hearing God's truth, deep in our heart.

DEAR GOD, PLEASE TEACH ME TO SPEAK THE RIGHT
WORDS AT THE RIGHT TIME WITH THE RIGHT TONE,
THAT I MAY LIVE IN PEACE AND HAPPINESS!

HEALING IS A MYSTERY

Healing is a mystery, a gift unknown,
A miracle that doctors have often shown.
With surgery, medicine, and gentle care,
They prepare the body to receive the repair.

Prepare yourself through faith and prayer,
Be open to creation's healing air.
In trust and hope, allow the power,
For healing blooms in its own hour.

Medicine works to spark the flame,
To heal the body, to soothe the pain.
Within us lies the Healer divine,
A force of love, a light that shines.

The surgeon humbly bows his head,
"I only attended," his wise words said.
For in the mystery, beyond our sight,
God's healing touch brings hope and light.

So embrace the mystery with open heart,
In faith and love, we play our part.
For healing's grace, a divine embrace,
In God's hands, we find our place.

SOMETIMES GOD USES PAIN TO INSPECT US, CORRECT
US, DIRECT US AND PERFECT US!

JESUS' LOVE

The love for equals is a simple grace,
A friend for a friend, a familiar face.
Brother for brother, sister for sister,
In love's embrace, our hearts grow crisper.

To love the less fortunate, a noble art,
For those who suffer, we open our heart.
The poor, the sick, the ones who mourn,
In compassion's arms, new hope is born.

The love for the fortunate, a rare delight,
To celebrate others' success without spite.
To rejoice with those who rise and shine,
Is a virtue both rare and divine.

And love for the enemy, a daunting call,
For those who mock and wish our fall.
This is the love Jesus showed,
A love that in kindness overflowed.

"Father, forgive them," he prayed on the cross,
In his suffering, he felt not loss.
For love that conquers the world is bold and true,
For it shines with a light so our hearts will renew.

WE AREN'T CALLED TO BE LIKE OTHER CHRISTIANS.
WE'RE CALLED TO BE LIKE JESUS.

CARRY HOPE WITH YOU

Carry hope with you through each day,
A light that guides you on your way.
Hope whispers softly of brighter skies,
That better things are on the rise.

In the toughest times, let hope remain,
A gentle reminder amidst the pain.
It tells you that you can persevere,
And overcome what you hold dear.

Hope assures you of your inner might,
Stronger than any challenge or fight.
It's a beacon shining in the night,
Reminding you to hold on tight.

Trust that you're exactly where you should be,
On the path meant for you, walking free.
Hope reassures you of your place,
In every step, a divine embrace.

Through every storm, let hope be your guide,
A faithful companion by your side.
In all these times, hope will see you through,
A steadfast friend, that's forever true.

SLEEP IN PEACE TONIGHT. GOD IS BIGGER THAN
ANYTHING YOU WILL FACE TOMORROW

Tuesday, March 25, 2025

EVERYTHING YOU LOVE

Everything you love with all your might,
Will love you back, still shining bright.
When it's right, the things you seek,
Will reach for you, strong yet meek.

In those moments, you'll understand,
Why some dreams slipped through your hand.
The hearts that failed to see your worth,
Were not your end, but your rebirth.

They didn't break, ruin or destroy you,
They built your strength, they made you true.
They taught you lessons, deep and vast,
Leading you to the love that lasts.

Shaping you with every turn,
Challenging you so you could learn.
Growing you through joy and pain,
To be the person you became.

So embrace the love you fiercely hold,
For it will return, more than gold.
In every challenge, see the light,
Guiding you to a love that's right.

WHEN GOD PUTS A TEAR IN YOUR EYE, IT'S BECAUSE
GOD WANTS TO PUT A RAINBOW IN YOUR HEART!

OUR STIFF NECKS

Our necks grow stiff from turning away,
Ignoring others' suffering, day by day.
How can we live in a throwaway place,
Where lives are valued less than a race?

A homeless soul lost on the street,
Ignored by headlines so never we meet.
Search engines don't speak their name,
Yet they daily suffer just the same.

Invisible faces on society's edge,
Struggling with poverty, and on the ledge.
Addiction, illness, disabilities too,
All hidden from view, out of the blue.

It's time to welcome, to open our door,
Provide shelter, love, and so much more.
Offer warmth to those in need,
A helping hand, and a loving deed.

Let's stop the cycle, let's break the chain,
Accept and love, ease the pain.
In hospitality, let our hearts unite,
Bringing hope and compassion, a guiding light.

THE WORLD OFFERS YOU A LOT OF EMPTINESS. GOD
OFFERS YOU A LOT OF PURPOSE.

LIFE'S TRUTH IS CLEAR

Life's truth is clear, it's not always fair,
Some face heartache, while others don't care.
A few strike it rich, but most do not,
We struggle with bills, our dreams often caught.

Rarely are we rich, beautiful, and strong,
Most of us are ordinary, trying to belong.
We face life's trials, health issues too,
A lesson learned early, and is often true.

Is God fair? No, God is more,
Generous in ways we can't ignore.
Life itself is a gift so grand,
Loved into existence by God's hand.

"Thank you, God, for loving us into life,"
A retreat master's prayer amidst the strife.
God's generosity knows no bounds,
In every moment, His love surrounds.

So embrace life's gifts, both big and small,
God's generosity, is a blessing to all.
In a world unfair, His love is clear,
A generous God, is forever near.

LIFE IS NOT ALWAYS FAIR, BUT GOD IS ALWAYS
FAITHFUL!

Friday, March 28, 2025

THE QUIET

We resist the quiet, keep screens aglow,
Fearing silence and the thoughts that flow.
We seek distraction, professionals as guides,
Ignoring the peace that within us abides.

We need to build in time for prayer,
To relax, reflect, and show we care.
Jesus took time to pray and rest,
Finding strength in God's love, always blessed.

To yield to God's power, we must be still,
Free from distractions, open to His will.
In quiet moments, we find our might,
Empowered by God's guiding light.

Let us learn to set aside our fears,
Embrace the silence, wipe away our tears.
In God's presence, we are refreshed,
Strengthened by His love, forever blessed.

Then, with His power flowing through,
We can help others, in all we do.
For in quiet, we find our grace,
Empowered by God's loving embrace.

SOMETIMES ALL IT TAKES IS ONE PRAYER TO CHANGE
EVERYTHING!

GOD'S IMAGE

Who bears God's image, who holds His light?
You and I do, when we are shining bright.
We're made in His likeness, created with care,
Belonging to God, His love that we share.

In our very being, we find the call,
To give back to God, to give our all.
This is my goal, my earnest plea,
To return to God what's been given to me.

I seek to give back, with heart and soul,
For in God's image, I am whole.
A reflection of love, a mirror of grace,
In giving back, I find my place.

Our lives are a gift, a divine embrace,
In God's presence, we find our space.
With each act of love, each selfless deed,
We give back to God, fulfilling our creed.

So let us remember, in all we do,
God's image in me and God's image in you.
With hearts open wide, let love abound,
Giving back to God, where true joy is found.

WHEN YOU WORK, YOU WORK.....WHEN YOU PRAY, GOD
WORKS!

Sunday, March 30, 2025

THE PHARISEES

The Pharisees followed the rules so tight,
But Jesus taught love was the guiding light.
Faith, he said, is not in rules confined,
But in loving God with heart and mind.

To love thy neighbor as you love yourself,
Is the greatest treasure, the truest wealth.
For when you know and love God above,
Your life will be filled with endless love.

Rules will come naturally to those who care,
Inspired by the love, they're eager to share.
Not just appearances, but deeds so kind,
For in loving actions, God's truth we find.

We too often fall in the Pharisees' way,
Focusing on rules that lead us astray.
Instead, seek relationships true and deep,
In love's warm embrace, our souls will keep.

So let us not be like Pharisees of old,
But live in love, with hearts so bold.
For faith is a journey, a love story told,
In the light of God's love, we find our gold.

IT IS POSSIBLE TO BE TOO BIG FOR GOD TO USE YOU. BUT
YOU CAN NEVER BE TOO SMALL FOR GOD TO USE YOU!

SPENDING ETERNITY ABOVE

We speak of spending eternity above,
With God and Jesus, wrapped in love.
We long for joy that will never end,
Surrounded by family and every friend.

But what will eternity be without our shell,
Without our goods, in Heaven to dwell?
We're used to nurturing both body and soul,
But without our bodies, will we feel whole?

Entering a realm without worldly ties,
No earthly goods to claim as a prize,
It's daunting, yet we trust in the Lord,
That His love will be our ultimate reward.

Will I see how my actions made a mark,
Beyond my tight circle, igniting a spark?
A special place in the world's vast plan,
For each unique woman and man.

To meet each soul from times of yore,
In Heaven's embrace, forevermore.
Sharing stories, love, and our light,
In the presence of Jesus, day and night.

WHEN GOD CREATED YOU, GOD CREATED A DREAM AND
WRAPPED A BODY AROUND IT,

WHAT MERCY LOOKS LIKE

What does mercy look like in our day?
It's the choice to listen and not turn away.
When the waitress seems overwhelmed and slow,
Mercy chooses patience, and lets compassion show.

When wronged, mercy doesn't make it tough,
For the one who seeks forgiveness, the path isn't rough.
It forgives so quickly, freeing the heart,
Creating a safe space for a new start.

Mercy allows questions and admits mistakes,
Giving the benefit of the doubt, for others' sakes.
It doesn't glare or send a harsh stare,
But offers kindness, choosing to care.

I act mercifully when I use my might,
To bring kindness and love, to do what's right.
Mercy empowers, transforms the day,
In simple acts, it lights the way.

May we all become people of grace,
Bringing mercy and love to every place.
For in each act of mercy we find,
A better world for all humankind.

STOP REMEMBERING WHAT GOD HAS FORGOTTEN!

Wednesday, April 2, 2025

OUR FIRST PRIORITY

Our first priority is God above,
In His voice and presence, we find true love.
If life is too busy to hear His call,
We're missing the greatest gift of all.

Service in God's kingdom should be our aim,
If we're too busy, it's a loss, not a gain.
Remember that one day, when time is through,
Our bond with God is all that will matter, too.

Invisible treasures are what truly last,
Earthly riches fade, like shadows cast.
Only the unseen is essential, we find,
In God's presence, there's true peace of mind.

The secret to living a life of grace,
Is making room for God, finding your place.
Reserve your time at His heavenly feast,
And all other worries will surely cease.

In eternity, where our souls will dwell,
Our relationship with God will tell.
So make Him your focus, your guiding star,
And in this life, you'll really go far.

ETERNITY IS A LONG TIME TO BE WRONG!

Thursday, April 3, 2025

MOST PEOPLE ARE GOOD

Most people are good; they care and they try,
They visit their loved ones and never ask why.
Even when time is tight and days are long,
They stop for a chat, where they feel they belong.

When friends fall ill, most people will call,
To check in and listen, to be there for all.
They give what they can, when money is scarce,
A testament to kindness and the love they share.

They worry about strangers they've never met,
In thoughts and prayers, their care is set.
In a world that seems dark, remember this truth,
That love and compassion aren't myths of our youth.

Most people, they strive to do what is right,
To make a difference, and to shine a light.
Amidst all the chaos, the goodness persists,
A reminder that humanity truly exists.

So when you feel weary and lose all hope,
Think of the good people, and how we all cope.
For most people are kind, with hearts so pure,
In their acts of love, you can always be sure.

THE THINGS YOU TAKE FOR GRANTED, SOMEONE ELSE IS
REALLY PRAYING FOR!

LIKE MUMMIES

Like mummies wrapped in layers tight,
We stay cocooned, avoiding the light.
Afraid to leave our tombs of fear,
To walk in faith, to draw God near.

We bind ourselves with doubt and pride,
And in our shells, we choose to hide.
The thought of change can bring alarm,
We cling to what we know as calm.

But Jesus calls us from the grave,
To live a life that's bold and brave.
He sets us free from the bonds we wear,
And gives us strength to truly care.

Faith and service, He demands,
Commitment in His guiding hands.
Obedience to His loving voice,
To step beyond our fearful choice.

So let us shed our wrappings tight,
And walk with Jesus in the light.
For in His love, we find our place,
A life of joy, of hope, and grace.

KEEP YOUR FEET ON THE GROUND, YOUR HEART ON THE
CROSS AND YOUR MIND ON HEAVEN!

Saturday, April 5, 2025

GOD GAVE US TWO HANDS

God gave us two hands, one for God, one for others,
To reach out to His people, our sisters and brothers.
If our hands are full, and struggling for greed,
We can't hold onto God or help those in need.

But if we hold onto God, who gave us our breath,
His love flows through us, defeating all death.
With one hand in His, and the other to share,
We'll find peace and joy, by showing we care.

When we let go of greed, we find room for grace,
In the warmth of His love, there's a beautiful place.
For the love that we hold in our hearts so true,
Will shine through our actions, in all that we do.

Our two hands were made for a purpose divine,
To connect with our Creator and let His love shine.
For the one who gives freely, with heart open wide,
Will find that love multiplies, and joy won't hide.

So, hold onto God, with faith strong and sure,
Reach out to your neighbor, your heart to endure.
For in this embrace, His love will grow grand,
Our maker gave us two hands, just as He planned.

IF YOU CAN TRUST A PUZZLE COMPANY TO MAKE SURE
EVERY PIECE IS IN THE BOX, WHY CAN'T YOU TRUST
GOD THAT EVERY PIECE OF YOUR LIFE IS THERE TOO?

SHOULD YOU GRIEVE

Should you grieve the passing of another weekend,
Think of the woman who never sees its end.
She works long hours, day by day,
To keep her family fed and her bills at bay.

Should your car break down in the middle of nowhere,
Think of those who can't walk anywhere.
A paraplegic dreams of taking a stroll,
While you lament your car's lack of control.

Should you spot a new gray hair in the mirror,
Think of the chemo patient without a glimmer.
She wishes for hair, gray or bright,
While she bravely faces her fight.

Should you question your life's grand design,
Be grateful for the moments you can call mine.
Many never get to ponder their fate,
Their time is cut short before it's too late.

Should you suffer from others' bitter views,
Remember, it's not your shoes they choose.
Their smallness and ignorance could be your lot,
But you walk your path, grateful for what you've got.

JESUS LOVES THE OUTCASTS. JESUS LOVES THE ONES
THE WORLD JUST LOVES TO HATE!

CLOSED MINDS

Closed-minded people refuse to hear
Another's point of view, or to draw near.
Quick with words or a sharp retort,
They silence others, leaving them short.

Disagreement is seen as a foe to defeat,
An enemy's voice they wish to delete.
Profanity flies, a shield and a spear,
To block out truths they don't want to hear.

Some believe that differing thought
Is an affront to God, a battle to be fought.
Yet wisdom comes when we choose to engage,
To listen, to learn, and not to enrage.

For the world is a canvas of colors, not one,
Each view, each voice, a part of the sum.
Embrace the challenge of a differing mind,
In understanding, we are truly intertwined.

Let hearts open wide and ears hear the plea,
For unity thrives in diversity.
So lay down the weapons of words and of war,
And open your heart to what others stand for.

AT THE END OF THE DAY, WHAT REALLY MATTERS IS
WHAT GOD THINKS OF ME!

Tuesday, April 8, 2025

THREE BIG SURPRISES

In heaven, three big surprises await,
The first, the people we didn't anticipate.
Shocked we'll be at who made it through,
"How did they get here?" we'll wonder anew.

The second surprise, a stark revelation,
Some saints we knew, won't be at their station.
Those we were certain had won the race,
Might not be seen in that heavenly place.

The third surprise, the greatest of all,
Is finding ourselves within heaven's call.
For who arrives, it's not our decree,
But the judgment of Christ, who sets us free.

Many claim to know the divine plan,
Of who gets to dwell in the promised land.
But in the end, it's not ours to decide,
It's Jesus who welcomes with arms open wide.

So let us live with hearts full of grace,
Encircling all with a loving embrace.
For heaven's secrets are not ours to tell,
But in love and kindness, we surely dwell.

YOU WEREN'T PUT ON THIS EARTH TO BE REMEMBERED.
YOU WERE PUT HERE TO PREPARE FOR ETERNITY!

STILL UNFINISHED

What's still unfinished in your life today?
So much remains as we live each day.
Life's tapestry is left unwound,
Interrupted by what's always around.

Most don't complete what they desire,
Our dreams are cut short by life's quagmire.
A bucket list we craft in haste,
Of all that we have yet to taste.

We hope to see our children grow,
Watch them shine, and let them know
Our love, our dreams, our deepest care,
In moments cherished, in moments rare.

We dream of weddings, and joyful sights,
Our grandchildren filling up our nights.
To finish work, to mend all our seams,
To heal old wounds, and fulfill old dreams.

Life's never done, it's always in flight,
A journey unfinished, from day to night.
We strive, we dream, we love, we try,
Completing our stories as we reach for the sky.

LORD, PLEASE SURROUND MY KIDS WITH FRIENDS AND
ADULTS WHO POINT THEM TOWARD YOU!

ASK THREE THINGS

To know a person's heart, just ask them three things:
What makes them laugh? What tears their heartstrings?
What stirs their anger, and makes them feel deep?
These are the secrets their soul does keep.

Today, we need not anger, but deep sighs,
The kind of sorrow that brings tears to our eyes.
Like Moses when he broke the sacred stone,
And climbed the mountain, for his people's sins to atone.

Or like when Jesus wept over the town,
His heart full of love as he gazed down.
It's easy to point at another person's disgrace,
But hard to look in the mirror and see our own face.

Anger is simple, it's a quick burning flame,
Yet anguish sits deeper, ever calling our name.
For anger without love won't heal our plight,
But hearts that are broken will guide us to light.

So let us learn from those with broken hearts,
And heal this world with the love that imparts.
Let's weep for our sins and then build anew,
A world full of laughter and hearts that are true.

BE WHO GOD WANTS YOU TO BE, NOT WHAT OTHERS
WANT TO SEE!

Friday, April 11, 2025

TWO TIMES WE CLEARLY HEAR

In life, there are two times we clearly hear,
A loving voice that draws us near.
As babies, it's our parent's sound,
That calms our cries as our fears abound.

In old age, a loved one's voice we seek,
To soothe our heart when times are bleak.
But none compare to Jesus' tone,
His voice is like peace, a love well known.

Amidst all the clamor, near life's end,
It's Jesus' voice that will surely transcend.
Inviting, warm, and full of grace,
A gentle guide to our rightful place.

We hope to follow, step in stride,
With faith in Him as our faithful guide.
To walk with Him, as our souls align,
Toward eternal life that is divine.

So let us listen, hearts wide and free,
To voices that guide us tenderly.
And strive to follow Jesus' call,
Our Shepherd, Savior, and Lord of all.

NOTHING DISPLAYS THE POWER OF CHRIST LIKE A
CHANGED LIFE!

Saturday, April 12, 2025

SPIRITUAL GROWTH

There are no shortcuts to spiritual growth,
No hand on the Bible to take an oath.
To bloom and become who we're meant to be,
Takes time, care, and a heart that's free.

We are the clay, in God's divine hand,
Shaping our lives with His gentle command.
Twisting and bending us, pounding the clay,
Through trials and triumphs, as we find our way.

Every event, both big and small,
Shapes us anew, and helps us stand tall.
In birth and death, in loss and gain,
God's loving touch removes our pain.

In each success and every fall,
God's presence remains through it all.
Each day a chance for us to see,
As God molds us into who we're meant to be.

God sent us Jesus, a beacon of light,
Guiding our steps through the darkest night.
With every moment, we strive to be,
More like Jesus, for all the world to see.

TODAY I WILL: 1. BE THANKFUL, 2. SEE THE GOOD IN
OTHERS, 3. TRUST GOD'S WAYS, 4. HAVE HOPE, 5. GO OUT
OF MY WAY TO BLESS SOMEONE!

Sunday, April 13, 2025

Palm Sunday

THE PALM AND THE PASSION

A piece of palm, a story told,
Of Christ's last days, both brave and bold.
We wave the palm, His triumph near,
"Blessed is He," the crowd would cheer.

The palm, so small, we take it home,
A symbol of the days to come.
It hangs behind our cross with care,
A sign of love beyond compare.

Yet soon the story turns to pain,
A Passion that we can't contain.
For suffering comes to every heart,
And death, for all, must play its part.

Jesus faced it, bold and true,
The cross before Him, suffering too.
In His example, we find the way,
To face our trials, day by day.

The palm and Passion, hand in hand,
Teach us what we must withstand.
For Christ's own death, and what He gave,
Shows us the path beyond the grave.

NOTHING IN MY WORLD CAN SATISFY MY SOUL LIKE
JESUS

Monday, April 14, 2025

EIGHT DAYS OF WONDER

Eight days of wonder, eight days of grace,
A story that time can never erase.
From Sunday's cheers of "Hosanna!" bright,
To Sunday's dawn, with a rising light.

Jesus rode on a donkey, humble and low,
As crowds with palms let praises flow.
On Monday, He cleared the temple square,
With righteous zeal, His heart laid bare.

On Tuesday, He spoke of the temple's fall,
A warning given to one and all.
Wednesday brought silence, a day of rest,
A pause before the coming test.

On Thursday, bread and wine were shared,
In an upper room, His love declared.
On Friday, death upon a tree,
For all humankind, Jesus set us free.

On Saturday, he lay in the grave,
A world in mourning, silent, and brave.
But Sunday came, the stone removed,
And Christ arose, His love now proved.

JESUS, JESUS…..YOU MAKE THE DARKNESS TREMBLE!

"MOURN, MY PEOPLE, MOURN"

"Mourn, my people, mourn," let your sorrow rise,
Burst forth with sobs and heartfelt cries.
Mourn the silence between you and your mate,
The unspoken words, the love turned to fate.

Mourn for innocence lost, stolen away,
The childhood dreams that could not stay.
Mourn the absence of a soft, warm embrace,
An intimate friendship, such a cherished place.

Mourn the inadequacy of this earthly strife,
Where all symphonies are unfinished in life.
Mourn for the hurts you've caused, the pain,
The love that's marred by sorrow's stain.

Mourn what might have been, the dreams that died,
The moments missed, the paths untried.
Mourn the gratitude that's lacking, unseen,
Taking for granted what should have been keen.

Mourn the blindness to gifts freely given,
The charity owed, yet often riven.
"Mourn, my people, mourn," for in this we find,
The depths of our hearts, and a soul more kind.

JESUS THOUGHT YOU WERE WORTH DYING FOR.
REMEMBER THAT!

Wednesday, April 16, 2025

WHEN CHRIST DID THE LEAST

In Christ's life, a curious design unfolds,
A pattern of activity, then passivity, it holds.
From ministry's start till the night of his strife,
He gives, he heals, and brings new life.

Active, he teaches, prays, and feeds,
Consoles the broken, meets their needs.
He works miracles, the doer's goal,
While others only play a smaller role.

Then in the garden, he's taken away,
From active deeds, he cannot sway.
In his passion, he becomes passive, still,
To others' actions, he bends his will.

Arrested, tried, and led to the cross,
In these final hours, all seems lost.
Yet in his passivity, salvation's wrought,
Through his suffering, redemption is brought.

Curious and ironic, it stands clear,
When Christ did least, salvation was near.
His passive hours, the most profound,
In helplessness, our hope was found.

WE LIVE AND DIE…..JESUS DIED AND LIVED!

Thursday, April 17, 2025

Holy Thursday

BROKEN BREAD GIVES US JESUS

Jesus took bread, broke it and said,
"This is my Body," for you, it's spread.
He took a cup, filled with wine,
"This is my blood, a gift divine."

He gave and shared Himself that day,
And continues to give himself in every way.
Jesus saves us, a truth profound,
In brokenness, His love is found.

Broken like the bread we take,
In every piece, His promise we make.
Broken soil produces crops so fair,
From the broken clouds, rain fills the air.

Broken bread gives us Jesus, pure,
A broken Jesus, our salvation is sure.
But we must admit to our broken state,
To find His grace, to meet our fate.

In our sins, our flaws, our pain,
Through our trials, His love we gain.
For in brokenness, we truly see,
The path to Him, and the way to be.

WHAT WOULD YOU DO IF YOU HAD JUST ONE DAY TO
LIVE? JESUS WASHED FEET!

Friday, April 18, 2025

Good Friday

HEY MAN ON THE CROSS!

"Hey, Man on the Cross! Why hang there so long?
Don't you wish to be free again and strong?
Two thousand years, your arms must ache,
Your heart so weary, your soul must break.

Hey! Man on the Cross, can you still see,
All the pain and wars, all the misery?
People lost, millions flee from their home,
While you remain, so still, so all alone.

The world's consumed with wealth and greed,
So many lost, so many in need.
We need you now, to walk our streets,
To teach us love where hatred meets.

Your crown of thorns, it must be sore,
Let me help you, and ease the gore.
But wait, I see, it's not the nails,
That bind you there through life's travails.

It's love that keeps you on that tree,
A love so great, it's now clear to me.
Hey! Man on the Cross, now I know,
Your love's the reason you won't go.

JESUS DIDN'T HAVE TO DIE ON A CROSS, BUT JESUS
LOVED YOU THAT MUCH. ALL JESUS ASKS IS THAT YOU
LOVE HIM BACK!

Saturday, April 19, 2025

Holy Saturday

THE WAY OF THE TOMB

Some of us stay at the cross so near,
Clinging to sorrow, holding our fear.
We weep for the pain that our Savior bore,
And miss His Risen life forevermore.

Some of us wait by the tomb in gloom,
Mourning the darkness, awaiting doom.
But if He had stayed beneath the stone,
Victory's power would remain unknown.

For Christ, though buried, did not remain,
He rose with triumph, broke every chain.
The tomb was but the passing door
To life eternal, forevermore.

The way of the tomb leads beyond defeat,
To a grace that makes all joy complete.
In the heavenly place where Christ ascends,
The story of hope and life never ends.

So rise with the Lord, victorious and free,
For death has no sting, no victory.
Our Savior lives, forever to reign,
His triumph is ours, and love will sustain.

EARTH'S SADDEST DAY AND GLADDEST DAY WERE
ONLY THREE DAYS APART!

Sunday, April 20, 2025

Easter Sunday

THE RISEN LORD IS ALWAYS NEAR

How many woke this Easter day,
With joy and wonder on display?
Yet some of us felt lost, alone,
Crabby, restless, on our own.

But Easter isn't just a mood,
It's faith, not feelings, that intrude.
The joy of Christmas, soft and bright,
Is different from Easter's sacred light.

For Easter holds a deeper call,
An empty tomb, a love for all.
A Risen Christ, alive and true,
Inviting us to a life anew.

Like Mary by the tomb, we stand,
Alone, but held by Jesus' hand.
We seek His face, and there we see,
That we are loved eternally.

So shake yourself from doubt and fear,
The Risen Lord is always near.
This is the moment, your faith is reborn,
With Jesus by your side each and every morn.

THE FIRST EASTER TAUGHT US THAT LIFE NEVER ENDS
AND THAT LOVE NEVER DIES!

JESUS IS ALIVE

Jesus is alive! We must remind our hearts,
Not a distant memory, but where our hope starts.
Not just a figure from ages long ago,
But living and present, calling us to follow.

If we see Jesus as a figure from the past,
We miss the power of a love so vast.
For He saved us then, and He saves us now,
His grace and love is in every vow.

Today Jesus fills us with grace so divine,
Liberates our souls, for in His love we shine.
He heals and consoles, with a touch so true,
The Risen Christ, making all things new.

He is not just a story, but our life's guiding light,
He's present in our lives, both day and night.
Jesus said, "I'll be with you, until the end of time,"
A promise so precious, it's eternally sublime.

So let's hold fast to this truth each day,
Jesus is alive, in each and every way.
He fills our hearts, He dispels the night,
Our Risen Savior, is our source of delight.

JESUS ISN'T ASKING YOU TO FIGURE IT ALL OUT. HE'S
ASKING YOU TO TRUST THAT HE ALREADY HAS!

JESUS BROUGHT A REVOLUTION

There have been many revolutionaries in history,
But none like Jesus, whose force is no mystery.
A revolution so deep, it transformed the heart,
Changing the world, setting it apart.

Historical revolutions changed systems and lands,
Political and economic shifts by human hands.
But none truly altered the soul's inner part,
None have the power to change the heart.

Jesus brought a revolution, profound and true,
Through His life, His love, and all He knew.
His resurrection brought light, broke every chain,
A change so immense, it's here to remain.

Unless Christians are revolutionaries, hearts aflame,
They miss the essence, of Christ and His name.
To be Christian is to embrace His radical way,
To live His unconditional love each and every day.

Through His resurrection, the world is reborn,
A dawn of hope, and a new bright morn.
Let's carry His message, be bold and be strong,
As revolutionaries of His love, is where we belong.

EASTER IS GOD SHOWING US THAT LIFE AT ITS CORE IS
SPIRITUAL AND TIMELESS!

THE ONLY EASTER SOME WILL SEE

Jesus calls us to be witnesses true,
To His Resurrection, in all we do.
Not "pew potatoes," sitting still,
But vessels of His love, His holy will.

We are not pious ghosts, unseen,
But living bodies, ever on the scene.
Like Jesus, we bear our scars,
Symbols of love, His guiding stars.

We are to threaten the world with life,
With the resurrected Jesus, to end the strife.
To bring His light to every place,
Reflecting His glory, His boundless grace.

The only Easter some will ever see,
Is the Jesus they see in you and me.
Through our actions, words, and care,
His resurrection, we surely declare.

We are His witnesses, strong and bold,
Sharing His story, new and old.
So rise, dear souls, with purpose clear,
Spread His message, both far and near.

TAKE CARE OF YOUR LIFE AND JESUS WILL TAKE CARE
OF YOUR DEATH!

THE PASCAL MYSTERY

It's cruel to speak of death, it's true,
But crueller still to silence it, too.
For adult life, unlike a child's play,
Asks us to die in our own way.

Physical death's just a part,
But we die daily, from the start.
Letting go of youth and health,
Of dreams and loves, our inner wealth.

No one lets go without a fight,
We deny, pretend with all our might.
Clinging to the life that we know,
Afraid to let our spirits grow.

Mary Magdalene, on that Easter morn,
Wanted Jesus as she'd known him before.
Yet the resurrection calls to her and us,
With death, a new life, for in God we trust.

The paschal mystery we embrace,
In death's shadow, is a new life's grace.
Through our struggles and our strife,
We find rebirth, and eternal life.

WE OUGHT TO BE LIVING AS IF JESUS DIED YESTERDAY,
ROSE THIS MORNING AND IS COMING BACK THIS
AFTERNOON!

Friday, April 25, 2025

RESURRECTION CALLS US

The resurrection is more than Christ's rise,
It's life's rebirth under open skies.
New life springs from winter's cold grip,
From all that's died, drip by drip.

Like nature needs spring every year,
We crave resurrections to draw near.
Parts of us lie frozen, crucified,
Awaiting the thaw where life's revived.

Life and death, in us they blend,
Not in God, where there's no end.
To live with death is easy to do,
Just turn your back on life's soulful view.

It's possible to be dead inside,
Unaware, of where our sorrows reside.
Asleep yet thinking we're awake,
Loving as our hearts begin to break.

Resurrection calls us to unthaw,
To let the child in us cry and be raw.
Open to new possibilities so bright,
Surprised by life, in spring's warm light.

THE RESURRECTION GIVES MY LIFE MEANING,
DIRECTION AND THE OPPORTUNITY TO START OVER, NO
MATTER WHAT MY PROBLEMS ARE!

THE LORD TAKES HIS TIME

God has not set a time for when He intervenes,
In our lives, He moves in ways unseen.
One way today, another tomorrow,
In every joy and in every sorrow.

The Lord chooses His way, gentle and kind,
Entering our lives with His purpose in mind.
Often He moves slowly, so slowly it seems,
We're in danger of losing patience with our dreams.

The Lord takes His time, He has patience so vast,
He waits for us, through each moment cast.
Even to the end, His love does not wane,
He waited for the Good Thief, through joy and pain.

The Lord who walks with us, at our own pace,
His patience abundant, His enduring grace.
In every step, He matches our stride,
With endless patience, He stays by our side.

So when life feels slow, and doubts arise,
Remember His wisdom, His caring eyes.
For God's timing is perfect, His plans are divine,
In His boundless patience, our spirits align.

WHEN YOU ARE DOWN TO NOTHING, GOD IS UP TO
SOMETHING!

THOMAS DOUBTED

Thomas doubted, he sought to see,
The risen Christ, His wounds to be.
He longed for proof, for touch, for sight,
To calm his heart and make things right.

I understand his longing cry,
For seeing truth with my own eye.
To touch, to hold, would make it real,
And help my heart to truly feel.

But faith is passed from heart to heart,
Through witnesses who do their part.
It's not by sight that truth takes hold,
But trust in stories shared and told.

Jesus calls the blessed ones near,
Not those who see, but those who hear.
Who leap in faith, though proof be thin,
And find His love alive within.

We may not touch His hands and side,
But in His Body we confide.
In every heart, in every prayer,
The Body of Christ is always there.

THE RESURRECTION OF JESUS CAN'T BE PROVED. JESUS
HIMSELF NEVER WANTED IT PROVED. JESUS ALWAYS
WANTED FOLLOWERS, NOT DETECTIVES!

SPRING REMINDS ME

Spring reminds me it's never too late,
To start anew, to change my fate.
Quiet growth in winter's embrace,
Hidden beneath the soil, is a sacred space.

Tulips bloom in the front yard, so bright,
Buds on the trees, a beautiful sight.
Voices of birds, the cleansing rain,
The comfort of sunshine after winter's pain.

Each gift renews me, day in and day out,
Awakening my senses, prompting me to shout.
As spring stirs my body, heart, and mind,
May God's touch awaken the dreams I find.

May my mind open up and blossom anew,
To the longings within, ever pure and true.
With spring's gentle whisper, my soul does sing,
Embracing the hope within that I hear calling.

With every dawn, let my spirit rise,
Reflecting the beauty of spring's bright skies.
In the warmth of the sun and the dance of the breeze,
May I find strength and peace, here on my knees.

THERE IS SOMETHING VERY COMFORTING ABOUT A
BILLION STARS HELD STEADY BY A GOD WHO KNOWS
WHAT HE IS DOING!

AWAKENING THE MYSTERY

Mystery unfolds when we let life evolve,
Not forcing its hand, but letting it solve.
It's a knock at the door, a blooming flower,
An afternoon in the yard, a quiet hour.

Just to see, just to notice, just to be there,
Mystery awakens with a gentle care.
It stirs our souls to something new,
A smell, a taste, a moment's view.

Locking eyes with a stranger in passing light,
A reminder of glory, a most wondrous sight.
Moments of astonishment, presence so divine,
Awareness of the unseen, a sacred sign.

For in the essence of mystery, we find,
Something wonderful, a treasure to bind.
At any moment, a miracle can start,
Awakening the mystery within our heart.

So let life flow, with its twists and turns,
In each surprise, a lesson learns.
For in mystery's embrace, we truly see,
The presence of God, and what life can be.

YOU CAN'T EXPECT GOD TO BE THE SOURCE OF YOUR
PEACE IF THE WORLD IS THE SOURCE OF YOUR
SATISFACTION!

LIFE IS A MOSAIC

Every life is simply a series of lives,
Each one with its task, where growth thrives.
Its own flavor, and its own brand of error,
Its own type of sin, and its own kind of terror.

Each life has its glories, its moments of despair,
A plethora of possibilities, forever waiting there.
All designed to lead us to the same end,
Happiness and fulfillment, where spirits ascend.

Life is a mosaic, made of many pieces,
Each full in itself, as the journey increases.
Every step a new beginning, a chance to explore,
A stepping stone to what's next, opening a new door.

With every mistake, and every triumph we see,
We craft our own path, towards who we will be.
Each fragment of life adds to the whole,
Forming a picture, enriching the soul.

So embrace every moment, every joy, every strife,
For they are the colors that paint your life.
In the mosaic we build, with love as our guide,
We find our true selves, with nothing to hide.

GOD CREATED YOUR LIFE. AND YOU'RE IN CHARGE TO
COLOR IT. MAKE IT BEAUTIFUL!

Thursday, May 1, 2025

ST. JOSEPH'S LEGACY

St. Joseph's legacy stands so clear,
In silent trust, God's voice he'd hear.
Not one word spoken in the Bible's span,
He's a man of action, God's faithful man.

He shows that destiny can be,
In supporting roles, his strength we see.
For another's rise, we play our part,
With quiet strength and a faithful heart.

In every act, his trust displayed,
In love and patience, always unafraid.
No need for words, his life proclaimed,
With God's guiding hand, his soul inflamed.

Our lives can mirror Joseph's way,
In humble deeds, our love convey.
So as we search, we will surely find,
In us, a strength, and a heart aligned.

For when we trust in God above,
Our actions speak with silent love.
Like Joseph, may we ever be,
Faithful, strong, patient and free.

PEOPLE JUDGE US BY THE SUCCESS OF OUR EFFORTS.
GOD LOOKS AT THE EFFORTS THEMSELVES!

Friday, May 2, 2025

THE ROSARY'S BEADS GUIDE ME

In quiet moments, I kneel to pray,
The rosary's beads guide me each day.
The Joyful Mysteries bring delight,
With scenes of love and holy light.

The Annunciation, humble and true,
Mary's "Yes" brought life anew.
The Visitation, joy's embrace,
And Jesus born in a lowly place.

But Sorrowful Mysteries touch my soul,
The Agony, where pain takes its toll.
The thorns, the cross, the heavy weight,
Christ's suffering and death, so deep, so great.

The Glorious Mysteries shine so bright,
With Resurrection's morning light.
The Ascension, and Pentecost's fire,
Mary's Assumption lifts us higher.

Each mystery, a bead of grace,
A prayer, a step, to God's embrace.
In every prayer, a sacred call,
I find His love within them all.

MAKE YOUR PRAYERS BIGGER THAN YOUR FEARS!

THE SHAPE OF OUR WORLD

We are responsible for the shape of our world,
Though it seems to reshape, and is often unfurled.
Why should we bother? The reason is clear,
The young and the old depend on us here.

We forever rely on them for life's many creations,
Products, inventions, and institutions' foundations.
They look to us to be their spiritual guide,
Having an understanding of life, from the inside.

Life always comes from the ashes of death,
The present is born from the past's final breath.
The future is bright for those who create,
A world of hope, where love does resonate.

We must confront fears, and stand brave and tall,
To become what God intended for us all.
In shaping the world with hearts pure and free,
We build a future, as God wants it to be.

So let us take hold of the task at hand,
Together we'll build a life that is grand.
For in unity and purpose, we find our way,
Creating tomorrow, from the ashes of today.

JESUS PROVED THAT THE WORST THINGS ARE NEVER
THE LAST THINGS!

Sunday, May 4, 2025

"DO YOU LOVE ME?"

The disciples fished on Galilee's shore,
Their hearts were heavy, they hoped no more.
Since the cross, their dreams had died,
They returned to the lives they'd left aside.

At dawn, a man stood by the sea,
But they didn't know who he could be.
He called, "Push out, cast your nets wide,"
And soon the fish were pulling inside.

The nets were full, they nearly broke,
In that moment, their hope awoke.
It's as if Jesus said, "Start anew,
I forgive, I am still calling you."

On the shore, they ate with Him there,
His mercy and love beyond compare.
For Peter, who denied Him thrice,
Jesus spoke words, gentle yet precise.

"Do you love me?" three times He asked,
And gave Peter a life-long task.
"Feed my sheep, tend to my fold,"
A calling of love, forever bold.

PRAY DAILY.....JESUS IS EASIER TO TALK TO THAN MOST
PEOPLE!

Monday, May 5, 2025

BREATHING CREATION

We can begin to make creation the spirit of our soul,
Breathe it in slowly, let it make us whole.
Let it saturate our hearts, open our eyes to see,
Parts of creation we've missed, so full of mystery.

We can decide to smile at everyone we greet,
To play with children, to make our joy complete.
To talk to seniors, ask questions and learn,
Listen to their stories, let our own hearts yearn.

We can pursue something new, embrace the unknown,
Become learners, feel excitement in seeds we've sown.
Let curiosity guide us, let passion arise,
Discovering the world with ever-widening eyes.

We can give ourselves to those who have no one else,
Offer our presence, our love, as our heart swells.
Be the support, the friend they need,
In every kind gesture, plant a loving seed.

For in these small actions, life's beauty we find,
In connecting with others, in being so kind.
A new beginning each day we start,
Breathing creation, with an open heart.

GOD GIVES US THINGS TO SHARE. GOD DOESN'T GIVE US
THINGS TO HOLD!

PATIENCE BRINGS PEACE

The more patient you are, the more you'll see,
Acceptance of life as it's meant to be.
Not insisting on ways that suit your desire,
But embracing each moment, no matter how dire.

Without patience, life is a constant strain,
Easily annoyed, and filled with pain.
Bothered and irritated by trivial things,
Frustration and anger that impatience brings.

Patience is key to inner peace,
A heart open wide, where troubles cease.
Seeing the innocence in others' eyes,
Opens your heart, to your surprise.

Don't mistake God's patience for His absence,
His timing is perfect, His love immense.
His presence is constant, always near,
In every moment, do feel Him here.

God is always with you, through thick and thin,
In every struggle, His love will always win.
Patience brings peace, a gentle embrace,
Guiding you softly with heavenly grace.

UNTIL GOD OPENS THE NEXT DOOR FOR YOU, PRAISE
GOD IN THE HALLWAY!

Wednesday, May 7, 2025

A CRY FOR THE WORLD

Oh Lord, I cry for the world, so torn,
For broken bodies, homes, and hearts worn.
I weep for the violence, the exclusion, the pain,
For the indifference that falls like cold, harsh rain.

Most of all, I cry for the children so dear,
That they have nourishing food, homes full of cheer.
May they find nurturing, in schools that are good,
Protected and hugged, as every child should.

Grant them the love and safety they need,
From every harm and every cruel deed.
Let them grow strong, in body and soul,
With vibrant dreams and hearts that are whole.

Oh Lord, hear my plea, see my tears,
Mend this world of its deep, deep fears.
Bring us together in compassion and care,
To heal the brokenness that is everywhere.

Let kindness flow in rivers so wide,
To wash away hatred, to bridge the divide.
With every prayer, with every heartfelt plea,
Oh Lord, bring us closer to unity and thee.

I WOULD RATHER STAND WITH GOD AND BE JUDGED BY
THE WORLD THAN STAND WITH THE WORLD AND BE
JUDGED BY GOD!

JESUS' LOVE FOR WOMEN

Jesus saw women as equals, true,
With respect and love, His kindness grew.
With gentle wit and honest care,
Their dignity was always in His prayer.

He genuinely liked them, it's clear,
With no exploitation, only sincere.
He was ever a model of maturity,
In His love, they found only purity.

Not once did He put a woman down,
In His presence, no need to ever frown.
No harsh words or blame He cast,
His respect for them was always steadfast.

In every tale the Gospels tell,
He treated women exceedingly well.
As full equals, He did see,
In His time, rare as it can be.

Such behavior stands out today,
A light in a world so often gray.
Jesus' love for women shines,
Timeless, true, in all confines.

SURE GOD CREATED MAN BEFORE WOMAN, BUT YOU
ALWAYS MAKE A ROUGH DRAFT BEFORE CREATING THE
FINAL MASTERPIECE!

A MOTHER'S HANDS

A mother's hands, now arthritic and worn,
With wrinkles etched by the years they've borne.
These hands once nimble, tender, and strong,
Have served with love so many days long.

They fed and bathed, they dressed with care,
Tied tiny shoelaces with patience rare.
Caressed and comforted through joys and pains,
In every moment, their tenderness remains.

These hands that prayed, with fingers entwined,
Seeking blessings, and peace of mind.
In silent whispers, faith was shared,
In every touch, they showed they cared.

Now aged and frail, their strength may fade,
But the love they gave is never frayed.
Her child kissed these hands, so dear,
The most beautiful hands ever so near.

For in each line and every crease,
Lives a story of love's tireless release.
A mother's hands, though changed by time,
Hold a beauty that's truly sublime.

THE LOVELIEST MASTERPIECE OF THE HEART OF GOD IS
THE HEART OF A MOTHER!

A MOTHER'S ROLE

Love leaves the dust in search of laughs,
Smiles at fingerprints, and tiny crafts.
Wipes tears before spilled milk is done,
Picks up the child before having fun.

Love reprimands, it guides with care,
Crawls with the baby, is always there.
Walks with the toddler, runs with the youth,
Stands aside as they seek their own truth.

Love's the key to a heart so pure,
Opens salvation's door for sure.
Before being a mother, a perfect home was pride,
Now giving roots and wings at her child's side.

Much to teach, a mother's role,
But love's the greatest, it fills the soul.
In every lesson, big or small,
Love's the answer, through it all.

So let us cherish a mother's love, day by day,
Love's gentle guidance, ever leading the way.
For in the end, it's love we leave,
A lasting gift we all receive.

"MOTHER" IS THE NAME FOR GOD ON THE LIPS AND IN
THE HEARTS OF LITTLE CHILDREN!

Sunday, May 11, 2025

Mother's Day

A MOTHER'S LOVE

This Mother's Day, let's reflect and see,
All the things mothers do so lovingly.
They bring us forth through miracle's way,
In a journey that's far from easy, they say.

Two decades they spend, preparing each meal,
Solving our problems, teaching us what's real.
Guiding us through the world's vast maze,
In countless loving, and patient ways.

They spend their lives with worry and care,
Even when gone, their love is still there.
Mother's Day can be tough, it's true,
For those whose mothers have bid adieu.

Yet their influence remains so strong,
In our hearts, they forever belong.
Their lessons, love, and tender touch,
Stay with us, meaning so very much.

So let's honor them, both near and far,
In every memory, they're our guiding star.
For a mother's love, forever stays,
Lighting our paths through all our days.

WITH A MOTHER'S LOVE, GOD WILL KEEP YOU FROM ALL
HARM. GOD WATCHES OVER YOU LIKE A MOTHER!

IN COMPETITION WE PUSH AND SHOVE

It's hard for us to truly love,
For in competition, we push and shove.
"Win! Be the best! Leave the others behind!"
Such thoughts infect our heart and mind.

From infancy, we're taught to strive,
To outdo others, to feel alive.
Our worth, we think, is in winning lies,
But with this belief, our love denies.

How can we love with hearts so cold,
When competition takes its hold?
To love means seeing others' worth,
In talents shared, we find new birth.

To love is to be vulnerable, it's true,
To see each other's point of view.
In Christ's mind, we find the key,
No more need to win, just unity.

Another's gifts don't pose a threat,
But they enhance our lives, a gift we get.
In Christ's embrace, we're all the same,
No one is above, no one to blame.

PUT GOD FIRST AND WATCH YOUR LIFE CHANGE!

Tuesday, May 13, 2025

THE MIRACLES AROUND US

Think about the first time you looked from a plane,
Saw the country sprawling, a vast terrain.
Maybe it was nighttime, with twinkling lights,
Cities and towns glowing, such a beautiful sight.

Or maybe it was daytime, with highways in view,
Rivers delineating the landscape true.
Didn't you feel a sense of wonder, so grand?
Thinking, "Wow! This is an unbelievable land!"

Along the way, we've lost this awe,
The wonder of flying, of life's grand draw.
We rush through days, we forget to see,
The miracles around us, so wondrously free.

Let's keep things in perspective, embrace the joy,
Remain thankful for the wonders that never annoy.
For in our present lives, so filled with grace,
Are amazing things we should never efface.

So look out the window, feel the thrill,
Let the wonder of life your spirit fill.
For every day is a gift, pure and bright,
In your unbelievable present, hold on tight.

EVERYWHERE I LOOK I SEE A TRACE OF GOD'S BEAUTY
AND GOD'S LOVING EMBRACE!

Wednesday, May 14, 2025

GOD, MOLD MY HEART

God, mold my heart into the form you desire,
Lead me to courage, ignite my inner fire.
Kindle the warmth in what's grown cold,
Energize my passions, let my spirit unfold.

Help me stand before life with a trusting heart,
With faith and openness, let discontent depart.
Instead of discontent, instill gratitude's grace,
In jealousy's place, may generosity embrace.

Replace judgment with compassion's gentle hand,
And in place of anger, let laughter ever stand.
Guide me, O Lord, through each and every day,
With love and kindness, show me your way.

Let my words be gentle, my actions be kind,
With a heart full of love, and a peaceful mind.
Teach me to see with eyes of empathy,
To feel the world's pain, and bring harmony.

In moments of doubt, be my guiding star,
Show me the path, no matter how far.
With trust in Your plan, I'll walk steadfast,
In Your love and mercy, my soul will ever bask.

WHEN LIFE PUSHES YOU TO THE EDGE, TRUST JESUS
FULLY. ONLY TWO THINGS CAN HAPPEN. EITHER JESUS
WILL CATCH YOU WHEN YOU FALL OR JESUS WILL
TEACH YOU HOW TO FLY!

Thursday, May 15, 2025

RICHES AND THINGS

Riches and things define the American dream,
We believe the more we have, the better we seem.
Sold on this agenda, it's part of our core,
To be blessed means to have and desire more.

The world and the Evil One push us to conform,
To pursue the agenda, that riches make us form.
When Christians define blessings by what they can hold,
The world wins the battle for our souls, we are told.

The "prosperity gospel" claims all should be rich,
But such slogans show the world's successful pitch.
May we focus on the Creator above all things,
Rather than be consumed by what wealth brings.

May we find our joy in the things God has made,
Not in material wealth, or in accolades.
For in His creation, true blessings abound,
In faith, love, and joy, true riches are found.

In seeking His kingdom, we find the true way,
To live blessed and full, every single day.
May our hearts find rest in His eternal love,
And seek the treasures that come from above.

WHEN YOU SEE GOD IN SMALL THINGS, YOU'LL SEE GOD
IN ALL THINGS!

Friday, May 16, 2025

THOUGH MILES APART

Life has its seasons, its ebb and flow,
A time for closeness, with joy to show.
Shared moments blessed, where hearts entwine,
In God's embrace, our spirits shine.

But life demands we move along,
Duty calls us with its steadfast song.
Farewells bring tears, a pained goodbye,
Yet in our hearts, we still stand by.

It's not as if we never met,
Our memories linger, free of regret.
What's shared becomes a greater part,
Of something vast within the heart.

Though miles apart, our spirits blend,
In silent nurture, we transcend.
Deep intimacy, a sacred thread,
Connecting us in the prayers we've said.

In Christ's great body, we unite,
Bringing forth consummation's light.
No distance dims the love we've known,
Together, yet apart, we've truly grown.

AS WITH THE SEASONS…..WHEN GOD GIVES YOU A NEW
BEGINNING, IT STARTS WITH AN ENDING!

Saturday, May 17, 2025

GOD'S GRAND DANCE

We nurse within our hearts a light,
A hope that we are special and bright.
Extraordinary, not by some chance,
For our lives are part of God's grand dance.

We long to know we're meant to be,
Not mere accidents, but by decree.
God's hand in our birth, we seek to find,
A cure for mortal woes, ever entwined.

When pressure mounts, we hide behind,
A vital lie, our fears so confined.
We fail to see the Good News' grace,
The gifts we crave are in their place.

Extraordinary, under divine care,
Precious lives beyond compare.
Not victims of fate or fleeting breath,
But cherished beings, defying death.

Our worth is not earned by worldly gain,
But by God's love, as we break the chain.
Created, loved, our lives attest,
It's in God's embrace, we find our rest.

PUT GOD FIRST AND WATCH YOUR LIFE CHANGE!

JESUS CALLS US TO LOVE

Jesus calls us to love, as He did first,
To quench the world's deep-seated thirst.
He loved when doubted, denied, betrayed,
In grace and mercy, His love stayed.

We're called to love without a gain,
To give without expecting a claim.
No strings attached, no rewards in sight,
Just love as Jesus showed His light.

We open ourselves to hurt and loss,
Just as He did upon the cross.
For love may wound, but still we try,
With hearts that trust and reach the sky.

We must love those not like us,
The ones who differ, who don't discuss.
For every soul, in Him, belongs,
And through this love, we grow strong.

Though it's not easy, it's what we're shown,
In love, we're never truly alone.
For Jesus loved us through our fall,
And now, He asks us to love all.

FRIENDS COME AND GO, BUT JESUS COMES AND STAYS!

A TENSION LIES

At the center of our lives, a tension lies,
A burning ache, a restless sigh.
Insatiable and deep, it never sleeps,
A longing within our hearts it keeps.

Sometimes it points to someone dear,
A love unfulfilled, we still hold near.
Other times, a goal we chase,
A yearning for a different place.

Most often though, it has no name,
An ache that's wild, it's hard to tame.
Restless spirits, filled with disquiet,
Searching for peace, but cannot buy it.

We long for freedom, boundless, vast,
A total embrace that holds us fast.
Our spirits urge us to explore,
To seek beyond, to crave for more.

Static we cannot, and will not be,
Our hearts compel us to be free.
In an endless search, our souls expand,
Ever reaching out for the infinite hand.

THE GOD WHO MADE YOU CAN ALSO REMAKE YOU!

HEALING AND PEACE

Healing and peace, they start to grow,
When warmed by gratitude's soft glow.
To banish bitterness and hate,
The fire of love must blaze, not wait.

Knowing we're loved, despite our sin,
Ignites the flame that burns within.
This gratitude, is a powerful light,
Dispels the wounds that plague our night.

With hearts revived by thankful grace,
We turn to prayer, seek God's embrace.
Our loyalties spread, our hearts expand,
In reconciliation, we take a stand.

To heal, we face our inner strife,
We confront the chaos in our life.
In helplessness, we seek God's hand,
In prayer, we find the strength to stand.

Bare and open, loved yet flawed,
We join with others, all loved by God.
Gratitude leads, and soon we find,
A healing and peace for heart and mind.

TRYING TO BE HAPPY WITHOUT A SENSE OF GOD'S
PRESENCE IS LIKE TRYING TO HAVE A BRIGHT DAY
WITHOUT THE SUN!

CONVERSION MUST BE RADICAL

Conversion must be radical, profound,
A revolution where new life is found.
If we were who we ought to be,
Then no need for drastic change, you see.

Evolution, always gentle and slow,
Would let our hearts and spirits grow.
But often we find, that's not the case,
We stumble and fall, in need of grace.

Immaturity, bad habits cling,
To a mediocrity they bring.
Without a change that shakes our core,
We fall into the same pits, more and more.

A sudden grace must intervene,
To cleanse us pure, to make us clean.
Extraordinary, bold, and true,
Only a conversion makes us new.

For in our hearts, is a deeper call,
To rise above, to ever stand tall.
Radical change, a life redefined,
Brings a revolution to the heart and mind.

GOD'S LOVE SUPPLY IS NEVER EMPTY!

Thursday, May 22, 2025

FACING WHAT'S REAL

Our culture struggles with the truth we seek,
To admit our flaws, to confess we're weak.
We rationalize, and make excuses with ease,
Demanding that standards bend to appease.

In prayer, honesty's a rare, fleeting flame,
Contrition's lost in the shadows of shame.
We fail to admit our sins, our wrong,
This temptation is deadly, yet so strong.

Not our sins, but denial's the worst of all,
The failure to rise and admit our fall.
More damaging than sin is this deceit,
It's a silent poison, subtle and fleet.

Self-honesty's the start of grace,
Admitting weakness, we find our place.
For sin unacknowledged blocks the light,
A sin against the Spirit, veiling the sight.

To heal, we must first face what's real,
Confess our sins, as we let the wounds reveal.
For in truth's embrace, we find our way,
To forgiveness, to light, and a brighter day.

THE PRESENCE OF GOD WILL NOT ALWAYS FIX YOUR
PROBLEMS, BUT IT WILL CLARIFY YOUR PERSPECTIVE!

AN ORDINARY LIFE

We live our lives in shadows cast,
In obscurity, our dreams held fast.
Our needs and dreams, much bigger than,
The lives we lead, the modest plan.

In small towns, we dwell each day,
No matter where our homes might lay.
Brief moments of joy, we catch a gleam,
But mostly wait for fuller dreams.

From this stems restlessness and strife,
A longing for a larger life.
To be the star, the name that's known,
Yet in the end, we're all alone.

Extraordinary, yet lives so plain,
This hidden life can bring us pain.
Unsatisfied, we crave a voice,
A chance to live, to make a choice.

But ordinary life can be enough,
If in Christ's path, we find our stuff.
In His hidden life, we find our way,
To peace and joy in every day.

AGING IS GOD'S IDEA. IT'S ONE OF THE WAYS GOD KEEPS
US HEADED HOMEWARD TO HIM!

LIFE BEGINS ANEW

In every second, life begins anew,
As countless souls both come and bid adieu.
In moments brief, the world does shift and spin,
With endless tales of virtue and of sin.

From joy to sorrow, in life's vast tapestry,
Each heart beats out its unique melody.
In every act, both grand and small, we find
The threads of fate that intertwine and bind.

Millions celebrate while others pray,
In silent hope or deep despair they stay.
Each story woven in the fabric tight,
In shadows dark or bathed in heaven's light.

Can we conceive a presence so divine,
That knows each hair, each silent tear and sign?
A love that spans the vast, unending seas,
And cares for all with tender, boundless ease?

Amidst the chaos, faith can light the way,
Believing in a God who sees us each day.
For in the smallest, quietest of things,
There lies a love that soars on unseen wings.

A RICH PERSON WITHOUT GOD IS JUST A POOR PERSON
WITH MONEY!

Sunday, May 25, 2025

THE SPIRIT WILL COME

Jesus had told them He would depart,
But the thought of loss weighed heavy on their heart.
They knew He was leaving, but not what it meant,
Still unsure of the path where they'd be sent.

Into this absence, the Spirit would come,
A gift from the Father, through His beloved Son.
The Advocate, present to guide and to lead,
Helping them love in word and in deed.

The Spirit would teach, as Jesus once taught,
To fill their hearts with wisdom they sought.
For though Jesus would no longer be near,
The Spirit's presence would calm their fear.

To love like Christ, they needed His grace,
To follow His call, they'd need to embrace
The Spirit's power, alive and strong,
To help them do right and fight against wrong.

Though Jesus was gone, they would not stand alone,
For the Spirit of truth had made them His own.
Guiding, teaching, forever by their side,
In love and faith, they would now abide.

YOU WOULDN'T BE ALIVE IF GOD DIDN'T HAVE A
PURPOSE FOR YOU. NO MATTER IF YOU ARE 30, 50 OR 95,
GOD STILL HAS SOMETHING FOR YOU TO DO!

Monday, May 26, 2025

Memorial Day

MEMORIAL DAY

It was a spring morn in eighteen sixty-six,
After the Civil War's devastating tricks.
Southerners marched, a sight profound,
To the cemetery, to solemn ground.

They decorated graves with care,
For both Union and Confederate there.
Mothers, daughters, widows too,
Burying hatred, and starting anew.

The healing time at last had come,
With flowers bright, their hearts not numb.
It marked the first Memorial Day,
In unity, they found the way.

Why is Memorial Day in May?
Because flowers bloom, a bright display.
With blooms to decorate each grave,
A gesture pure, to honor the brave.

So every year, when May is here,
We remember those we hold so dear.
With blooming flowers, graves adorned,
Their sacrifice, is forever mourned.

YOU WEREN'T PUT ON EARTH TO BE REMEMBERED. YOU
WERE PUT ON EARTH TO BE RE-MEMBERED IN HEAVEN!

IN EDEN'S GARDEN

In Eden's garden, pure and free from strife,
Where Adam and his Eve first breathed their life,
A simple choice led to a fateful fall,
And marked the start of human flaws and all.

Confronted by the Lord, they turned away,
In fear and shame, they could not simply say,
"We sinned," but chose to rationalize their plight,
And cast their blame within the dimming light.

"The woman gave me fruit," did Adam cry,
"The serpent tempted me," was Eve's reply.
A chance for honesty was left behind,
And human hearts to wounded ways consigned.

Had they but owned their sin with humble grace,
Admitted fault and sought the Lord's embrace,
Perhaps our path through time would different be,
A story marked by truth and clemency.

Yet still we follow in their shadowed trail,
Where lies and rationalizations pale,
We hide from what could heal and make us whole,
And deeper sink into the fractured soul.

GOD ANSWERS THE MESS OF LIFE WITH ONE WORD:
"GRACE!"

Wednesday, May 28, 2025

WE JOURNEY

We journey through our lives with struggle rife,
Each heart bears wounds, and endures the strife.
With dreams dashed and frustrations deeply known,
We often envy lives that are not our own.

In others' fortunes, we see what we lack,
And in their light, our lives we then attack.
Disappointment grows within our hearts,
And from our joy and peace, we drift apart.

Instead of living fully where we stand,
We put our dreams and hopes upon the sand.
We chase the things we think will make us whole,
Ignoring the treasures in our very soul.

We yearn for partners, friendships, fleeting fame,
Or beauty's grace, a well-respected name.
In chasing shadows, we forget to see,
The simple joys that make us truly free.

Let's pick up our lives and live them as our own,
With creativity and love that's fully grown.
For in accepting all we have to give,
We find the happiness that lets us live.

THE SMILE ON MY FACE DOESN'T MEAN MY LIFE IS
PERFECT. I JUST APPRECIATE WHAT I HAVE AND HOW
GOD HAS BLESSED ME!

Thursday, May 29, 2025

Ascension Thursday

THE ASCENSION

The Ascension saw Jesus rise,
Leaving earth for heavenly skies.
From mortal bounds, He took His flight,
To be the glorified Lord of eternal light.

Our loved ones, too, in death depart,
Leaving their bodies, but not our heart.
They reach the fullness of life above,
In heaven's embrace, in eternal love.

Two kinds of death we come to know,
As through this life we ebb and flow.
Terminal death, an earthly end,
To joys and sorrows, to foe and friend.

But seminal death, a deeper tale,
A loss that brings a life to scale.
A new spirit, a life that's reborn,
As day breaks after night forlorn.

The Ascension means Jesus paved the way,
To a seminal death for a brighter day.
To new life, found at heaven's door,
With Jesus, and loved ones evermore.

IT IS BETTER TO WALK WITH GOD THAN TO WALK WITH
A CROWD THAT IS GOING IN THE WRONG DIRECTION!

Friday, May 30, 2025

WHAT IS GOD SAYING?

God does not start the fires or floods,
Nor wars that spill our human bloods.
Nature, chance, and human sin,
Bring these trials that we live within.

Yet through these events, God speaks clear,
In joys and sorrows, both far and near.
Disasters strike, and blessings too,
In each, God's message shines through.

For farmers, accidents do not exist,
In providence, their faith persists.
A bountiful crop, a sign of grace,
A poor one, a call to embrace.

To live on less, is a prayer profound,
In every loss, God's voice is found.
Through accidents that shape our days,
God's guiding hand appears in countless ways.

In every event, big or small,
God's finger writes, we heed the call.
"What is God saying?" we inquire,
In life's chaos, we find the divine fire.

GOD, GIVE ME A LISTENING HEART!

Saturday, May 31, 2025

GOD BLESSES US STILL

Is our world good or bad, we ponder deep,
As through its tangled paths we often creep.
There's good in every corner, light and grace,
In secular realms, it's God's love we trace.

From nature's wonders to kind acts we see,
A moral strength shines bright for you and me.
God, author of all goodness, works within,
Blessing the world, despite its evident sin.

Yet, starkly clear, the cross of Christ reveals,
The world's rejection, the wounds that never heal.
In crucifixion's shadow, truth stands bare,
The weak betrayed, the world's dark heart laid bare.

God blesses still, with love and constant care,
Affirming all the good that's everywhere.
Yet Christ's cross stands, a judgment and a guide,
Exposing darkness where it tries to hide.

Both truths exist, in tension and in peace,
God's love and judgment, neither one can cease.
A world blessed and condemned, held in God's sight,
Where grace and truth both shine in endless light.

A HEART FILLED WITH LOVE FOR GOD HAS NO ROOM
FOR HATE!

Sunday, June 1, 2025

TO PRAY ALWAYS

To pray always, as Jesus taught,
Means seeing life's signs, as we ought.
In "accidents", God's hand we trace,
Reading providence, moments of grace.

The language of God, life's sacred art,
Writes into our lives, softening the heart.
Moments of grace, in vulnerability's light,
Bring tenderness, compassion's delight.

In our shared struggle, we find our place,
A common heart in the human race.
To see our connectedness, to feel the pain,
Is to soften the heart, and break the chain.

The world is hard, coldness can grow,
If tender moments we do not know.
Massage these moments, let them stay,
In prayerful hearts, they light the way.

A tender moment, simple and pure,
Makes us aware, our hearts can endure.
Our common wound, our common sin,
In need of grace, we all begin.

THE BEST WAY TO FIND LOVE IS TO FIND GOD!

Monday, June 2, 2025

A HEALTHY SELF

A healthy self, both strong and kind,
Embraces a care for heart and mind.
In balance found 'twixt love and give,
A fuller and richer life we live.

To serve with joy and not in spite,
We must ensure our hearts are light.
For love flows best when self is whole,
Receiving care to nourish our soul.

Yet giving all, as Jesus taught,
In self-renunciation sought,
We find a peace that's deep and true,
A happiness in all that we do.

Boundaries placed with wisdom's art,
Protect and nurture every part.
But in the giving, lives are found,
In selflessness, our joys abound.

Thus, health is found in balance fine,
To care for self, and yet, resign.
In loving others, we receive,
And through this grace, we truly live.

GOD LOVES YOU SO MUCH THAT YOU GET TO RUN YOUR
LIFE THE WAY YOU CHOOSE!

THE LIGHT THAT FOREVER LASTS

In the shadows, where the world turns gray,
Lie souls deemed unworthy by those who sway.
The sick, the frail, the broken and torn,
Yet through their cracks, the light is born.

Those with minds lost to time's cruel embrace,
Alzheimer's steals but cannot erase,
Handicapped souls with courage so vast,
They hold the light that forever lasts.

The unborn, silent yet profound,
In their potential, the light is found.
The poor with hearts of humble might,
They shine through the darkest night.

Compassion masked in mercy's guise,
Euthanasia, abortion, a compromise.
But snuffing hearts for dignity's name,
Is this progress or a hidden shame?

Wisdom falters, compassion bends,
When life's value, on judgment depends.
In cracks, the light enters, souls impart,
The true essence of a compassionate heart.

 I WANT TO ASK GOD WHY HE ALLOWS POVERTY,
FAMINE AND INJUSTICE IN THE WORLD WHEN HE COULD
DO SOMETHING ABOUT IT. BUT I'M AFRAID GOD MIGHT
JUST ASK ME THE SAME QUESTION!

Wednesday, June 4, 2025

TO SPEAK OF SOFTNESS

In a world so hard and tough,
Where success is deemed enough,
Professional airs and competitive might,
Leave no room for the soft and light.

Efficiency reigns, hearts turn to stone,
In workplaces and homes, softness is unknown.
A call for tenderness is seen as weak,
Respect and status, it seems, they seek.

Yet without a heart, the brain will wane,
A softening mind in a world so vain.
Everything conspires against the gentle touch,
Our lives grow cold, we lose so much.

To speak of softness is to take a stand,
Against the harshness that grips this land.
But sentimental hearts find little space,
In a world where toughness wins the race.

Oh, for a world where soft hearts prevail,
Where love and tenderness never fail.
A place where warmth and kindness thrive,
And in that softness, true strength's alive.

DON'T BE TOO BUSY TO NOTICE WHAT GOD IS DOING
ALL AROUND YOU AND DEEP INSIDE OF YOU!

Thursday, June 5, 2025

GUILT WHISPERS

In moments when joy feels so deeply right,
Guilt whispers, shadows joy with its slight.
As if each laugh or blissful sight,
Steals from the heavens their pure delight.

Pleasure's bloom, a garden in spring,
Yet in its midst, guilt's whispers sting.
For every smile, for every song we sing,
A debt we feel, an unknown string.

Deep inside, the pleasure's pure,
Yet thoughts of worthiness obscure.
How can joy be felt, so sure,
When shadows of guilt we endure?

Gift of life, time, love, and more,
Each one a treasure, a boundless store.
Yet with each gift, we feel the score,
A debt, a weight, we can't ignore.

So we give, in hope to balance the scales,
To quiet the guilt that ever assails.
In giving, the heart's song prevails,
Finding peace in love's true trails.

TELL YOUR MOUNTAIN ABOUT YOUR GOD!

OPTIMISM AND PESSIMISM

Optimism and pessimism, each a way,
Rooted in our temperaments, they say.
Yet for the Christian heart, they pray,
Hope is where our trust should lay.

Not in the light of cheerful days,
Nor in the darkness pessimists praise.
But in the power of God, always,
Where hope finds its steady gaze.

Hope's foundation isn't in our mood,
Nor in what seems practically good.
It's in belief that God's love is stood,
Infinite and gracious, as understood.

Peace and justice, community's thread,
Forgiveness, oneness, where hearts are led.
Not from mere positive thoughts spread,
But from God's power, in raising the dead.

In hope, we trust what God can see,
Beyond our limits, wild and free.
For in His grace, eternally,
All will turn out as it should be.

CHRISTIANITY IS NOT ABOUT BEHAVIOR MODIFICATION,
IT'S ABOUT HEART TRANSFORMATION!

INTERRUPTIONS

In life's swift course, our plans we make,
Yet interruptions cause hearts to ache.
A minor call or a major care,
Derails our path, our dreams are laid bare.

A parent's need, a sudden call,
Big or small, they stall us all.
With each demand, our plans denied,
Resentment grows, hope is cast aside.

"If only this hadn't come my way,
My dreams would shine, not fade to gray."
Yet in these twists, a hidden guide,
God's hand directs where dreams abide.

With us in control, we'd selfish be,
Empty of joy, no simplicity.
Without derailments in our way,
Our hearts might never learn to sway.

Yet sometimes gratitude finds a place,
Interruptions become our saving grace.
For in these moments, by life's design,
Comes our true agenda, God's divine.

THE ONLY WAY GOD CAN SHOW US THAT GOD IS IN
CONTROL IS TO PUT US IN SITUATIONS THAT WE CAN'T
CONTROL!

Sunday, June 8, 2025

Pentecost

UNLESS THE EYE CATCH FIRE

Unless the eye catch fire, God will not be seen,
In the light of vision, a divine serene.
Unless the ear catch fire, God will not be heard,
In the sound of whispers, a sacred word.

Unless the tongue catch fire, God will not be named,
In the heat of speech, the holy acclaimed.
Unless the heart catch fire, God will not be loved,
In the warmth of passion, from above.

Unless the mind catch fire, God will not be known,
In the blaze of thought, the seeds are sown.
Embrace this fire, let the spirit ignite,
In every facet, find divine light.

Let every sense awaken, in fervent desire,
Each in its essence, a flicker of fire.
With eyes that see, and ears that hear,
In heart and mind, God's truth draws near.

In the dance of flames, find your soul's intent,
In the Holy Spirit's fire, be wholly spent.
For only through fire, the divine is shown,
In every moment, let God's light be known.

PEOPLE ASK ME, "DO I NEED THE HOLY SPIRIT TO GET TO
HEAVEN?" YOU NEED THE HOLY SPIRIT TO GET TO WAL-
MART!

Monday, June 9, 2025

TO FIND TRUE PEACE

To find true peace, is a daunting quest,
Our hearts and minds are seldom at rest.
Complex and torn, in every way,
Contradictions dance, both night and day.

Within us lies a tangled thread,
Desires and thoughts, in chaos spread.
To live in peace, is a simple dream,
Yet harder than it might first seem.

Peace is more than the conflict's end,
It's harmony where elements blend.
A symphony within the soul,
Where every part plays its role.

We must unite each inner piece,
For only then will we find peace.
Each element, a friend must be,
In perfect, heartfelt unity.

Without this balance, life's too small,
A narrow space, no room at all.
But harmony, when it's achieved,
Gives life a fullness, and is well-received.

WHEN GOD COMES INTO YOUR LIFE, GOD LIGHTS A
CANDLE IN YOUR SOUL!

Tuesday, June 10, 2025

BUILT FOR THE INFINITE

We enter this world with minds and hearts,
Built for the infinite, yearning to start.
We ache for love, so vast and grand,
To embrace the world, with outstretched hand.

Inside our hearts, is a timeless beat,
Out of sync with the finite we meet.
Built for the infinite, we crave the whole,
Yet life offers pieces, never the soul.

We strive to be perfect, to reach for the skies,
But find our achievements blemished with sighs.
We yearn for the eternal, frustrated by time,
Our demands so high, in life's endless climb.

In relationships, jobs, vacations, we seek,
Perfection so elusive, it makes our hearts weak.
Frustration lingers, dreams seem slight,
The symphony unfinished, ever out of sight.

Without belief in a life beyond,
We demand this life be our perfect song.
One life we live, a tragic quest,
Unfulfilled, we struggle to finally rest.

TO LOVE ANOTHER PERSON IS TO SEE THE FACE OF GOD!

Wednesday, June 11, 2025

EMBRACE THE ORDINARY

Our lives seem too small, confined in their scope,
We yearn for significance, to kindle new hope.
The city we live in, our jobs and our friends,
Feel ordinary, domestic, with no greater ends.

Life feels so vast, while we seem so slight,
Seeking to leave marks, to shine a bright light.
Perhaps a baby, new life to impart,
A timeless creation, from the depths of our heart.

Yet, will this change bring more restlessness near,
Tied down by new bounds, unable to veer?
We fear growing smaller in a life so confined,
As the weight of new duties, on our shoulders aligned.

Present in moments, we discover what's rare,
In ordinary lives, we find love and care.
By cherishing the simple, we grow beyond bounds,
In the mundane and daily, profoundness resounds.

So, be present to life, in its quiet grace,
Embrace the ordinary, find your place.
In the simple and small, extraordinary is found,
And our small lives, with greatness are crowned.

IN A SOCIETY THAT HAS YOU COUNTING YOUR MONEY,
YOUR POUNDS AND YOUR CALORIES, BE A REBEL AND
COUNT YOUR BLESSINGS!

Thursday, June 12, 2025

OUR WORLDS' DEEP DIVIDE

Few cries are louder than our world's deep divide,
Hatred, anger, and ideologies collide.
Sincere hearts torn from one another,
Good from the good, brother from brother.

Truth stands divided, no common ground,
Good people, once close, now nowhere to be found.
Conversations cease, charity fades,
In the emotional schism, love degrades.

Hearts driven by ideology's might,
Blind to compassion, ever losing sight.
We are called to mend this rift,
To be reconcilers, love's true gift.

Jesus, today, would call us anew,
To hearts and minds ever-loyal and true.
To bear the pain, as he did on the cross,
Embrace the vulnerable, despite your loss.

Absorb the pain, let love remain,
In unity's name, heal the strain.
For in the end, it's love that mends,
And brings together foes as friends.

JESUS DOESN'T ONLY LOVE YOU. HE LOVES EVERYONE
YOU KNOW. SO TREAT THEM WELL!

CHILDREN PLAYING IN THE SUN

I could not hope for more delight,
Than seeing my children in sunlight bright.
Surely this wish, a parent's purest grace,
To watch their children in the sun's warm embrace.

Every mother and father, with hearts so true,
Arrange moments, if only a few,
For their children to bask in the day's warm run,
To play and laugh under the radiant sun.

Despite the flaws and struggles they face,
Parents know goodness in that sunny space.
In those moments, nothing more to be done,
But to see their children play in the sun.

God, the ultimate parent, understands this joy,
Watching His children, both girl and boy.
Nothing pleases God more, no greater fun,
Than seeing us happy, playing in the sun.

So let us cherish these moments of light,
For in them, our hearts take flight.
In the sun's warm glow, we become one,
Reflecting God's love, playing in the sun.

LIFE IS A SERIES OF THOUSANDS OF GOD'S MIRACLES.
DON'T MISS TAKING NOTICE OF THEM!

Saturday, June 14, 2025

Trinity Sunday

THE TRINITY IS LIKE THE SUN

The Trinity is like the sun in the sky,
God the Father is the sun blazing high.
Jesus is the rays that shine down bright,
Guiding us all with His holy light.

From Father and Son comes the Spirit's heat,
Warming our souls with a love complete.
Like sun and rays bring warmth to earth,
The Trinity shows us our true worth.

The sun sends rays to the world below,
Just as God sent Jesus so we might know.
In rays and warmth, we see the sign,
Of the Father, the Son, and Spirit divine.

In this mystery of light and heat,
God's love for us is made complete.
A unity in diversity, profound and true,
The Trinity's love, is forever new.

So look to the sun and feel its rays,
And remember the Trinity in all your days.
For in this wonder, both great and small,
God's eternal love embraces us all.

I BELIEVE IN THE TRINITY, LIKE I BELIEVE IN THE SUN .
BECAUSE OF THE SUN, I CAN SEE EVERYTHING ELSE!

Sunday, June 15, 2025

Father's Day

IF YOUR FATHER WAS PATIENT

We project on God the traits we see,
From those we admire, unconsciously.
Believing God treats us just the same,
As others do, we call His name.

If your father was patient, you find,
God's patience, too, is gentle and kind.
You feel God's concern in every part,
For you are cherished in His heart.

If your father was kind, you perceive,
God's gracious acts, His love to receive.
You feel His intervention, pure and deep,
In God's embrace, your soul will sleep.

If your father was giving, you may see,
God's support and generosity.
Believing God provides the best for you,
In return, you give your kindness too.

If your father protected you, it's clear,
God's protection, you hold dear.
Worthy under His care, you find,
In God's security, peace of mind.

GOD IS NOT ONLY THE DOCTOR WHO MENDS A BROKEN
HEART. GOD IS ALSO THE FATHER WHO WIPES AWAY
YOUR TEARS!

OUR ULTIMATE CALL

Show me a selfish heart that's truly glad,
For joy in giving is what we've always had.
Made in God's image, a fire burns bright,
Energy for love, creativity, and light.

Inside us, a restless, insatiable flame,
But not chaotic, it follows God's name.
Configured and clear, with purpose profound,
In patterns of meaning, our lives are bound.

We burn with God's fire, divine and pure,
To bless and to fight, to teach and ensure.
To create delight in hearts all around,
And to empty ourselves, where love is found.

To act like Christ, our ultimate call,
In selfless love, we give our all.
For in this fire, we find true grace,
In serving others, we see God's face.

No selfish soul can claim true peace,
For joy in giving will never cease.
It's in God's fire, with divine intent,
That happiness finds its true content.

GOD ALWAYS FINDS US IN THE HOLES WE DIG FOR
OURSELVES!

Tuesday, June 17, 2025

SOLITUDE AND SILENT PRAYER

God is found in solitude and silent prayer,
In moments alone, with no one else there.
Few progress spiritually without this space,
To meet with God in a quiet embrace.

Yet finding time is a challenge we face,
Good intentions often lose the race.
Daily silence, a struggle to achieve,
In busy lives, it's hard to believe.

Uneasy feelings, workaholics' plight,
No meaning found outside of their might.
But a gracious heart in response and care,
Can mirror the peace found in silent prayer.

A loving heart leads where God calls us to be,
In acts of kindness, we truly see.
The deep demands of God and love unite,
In service, we find our spiritual light.

So seek solitude, but also be aware,
A heart of love is itself a prayer.
In silence or service, God's presence is known,
In both, a spiritual life is grown.

GOD'S HAND NEVER LETS GO OF YOU!

A CONSTANT YEARNING

All life is fired by a constant yearning,
Plants and humans, ever learning.
To eat, to grow, to breed, to push,
An insatiable pressure, a restless hush.

At the heart of the soul, this longing lies,
A force unseen, beneath the skies.
What does it mean to yearn, to crave?
A drive so deep, it's what we save.

To eat, to drink, to love, to feel,
A pressure inside, so dark and real.
To be beyond our skins, immortal dreams,
An endless quest, or so it seems.

Mostly unconscious, this relentless force,
Driving our lives, charting our course.
A pressure to reach, to touch the skies,
To find the place where longing lies.

In every soul, this fire burns bright,
A quest for more, both day and night.
To yearn, to strive, to reach above,
A life defined by endless love.

MANY PEOPLE TURN TO GOD WHEN LIFE HAS THEM
DOWN, BUT THEY FORGET TO KEEP IN TOUCH WHEN GOD
TURNS IT ALL AROUND!

Thursday, June 19, 2025

OUR YOUNG ONES CRAVE

Our young ones crave our gaze so keen,
To feel seen and valued, and not unseen.
Deep inside, they yearn for our touch,
An adult connection, that means so much.

The surface might hide what they feel,
Impressions given, often not real.
They act as if they don't need us there,
But truth reveals their inner care.

"Leave us be," they might protest loud,
Yet in their hearts, they seek us proud.
Desperate for blessings our presence brings,
They need to feel the love that springs.

More than words, our gaze they seek,
Our seeing them makes their spirits peak.
Acting out, a silent plea,
"Notice me, let me be free."

So let's give our gaze, our time, our care,
Be present for them, and always there.
For in our eyes, they find their place,
A sense of worth, a warm embrace.

DON'T GIVE GOD INSTRUCTIONS…..JUST REPORT FOR
DUTY!

TO BE SINCERE

To be sincere, uncorrupted within,
In heart, mind, soul, free from sin.
Bare and naked, your true self shown,
Without pretence, your essence known.

Uncoated by whims or political sway,
Free from posturing, in truth you stay.
Without false props, no mask to wear,
Just pure and honest, nothing to spare.

The quest for sincerity, a journey deep,
To grow up fully, our soul to keep.
Resisting the immature, standing tall,
Facing ourselves, answering the call.

To be sincere is to shed all lies,
To see the world through clear, true eyes.
Meeting each other with hearts unmasked,
In God's pure light, our souls unasked.

Sincerity stands as the final guard,
Against the immature, it's always hard.
Yet in its struggle, we find our grace,
Facing truth, in each other's embrace.

DEAR JESUS. MAY YOUR LOVE BE MY COMPANION IN
THE WAR I FIGHT AGAINST MY EGO AND MY PRIDE!

Saturday, June 21, 2025

BUILT FOR ETERNITY

In this life, no symphony of ours is complete,
Our hearts, minds, souls are in infinite retreat.
Built for eternity, we ache inside,
Grand Canyons vast, with no end in sight.

Lonely, restless, we seek what's more,
Incomplete, in life's great grand store.
Tormented by what we can't attain,
Living with longing, amidst the pain.

Today, life after birth is what we prize,
While life after death slips from our eyes.
Childhood daydreams may fade and die,
But deep within, our feelings still fly.

Infinite caverns, feelings so vast,
Aching as much as in the past.
Ever knowing dreams that won't come true,
Yet this side of eternity, we still pursue.

Our hearts forever in a quest,
For something more, an endless test.
In life's embrace, we find no rest,
Eternal longing is our deepest pest.

MAN IS A CREATURE MADE AT THE END OF THE WEEK'S
WORK. GOD WAS TIRED!

THE BODY OF CHRIST

We are all one body, eight billion as one,
In God's eyes, our journey has just begun.
Not as ants on earth, in chaos unfurled,
But a single body, embracing the world.

When one feels pain, the whole body knows,
In sickness and health, the unity shows.
A headache, a fever, affects the whole,
For God sees us all, one interconnected soul.

The Body of Christ, a mystery profound,
In it, the divine unity is found.
Unlike other food that we consume,
In eating this Body, we find our true bloom.

For when we partake, we do not just eat,
We become the Body, in unity complete.
In Christ's embrace, we are transformed,
A divine union, in a spirit conformed.

So let us remember, in every breath,
We are one body, in life and in death.
Together in love, compassion we show,
In the eyes of God, as one we grow.

JESUS DIDN'T DIE AS A FAILED REVOLUTIONARY. JESUS' DEATH WAS THE REVOLUTION!

Monday, June 23, 2025

SETTING GOALS

Setting goals each day is key,
They keep us focused, they help us see.
Without goals, tasks would overwhelm,
But when limits are set, we take the helm.

Goals provide a clear-cut line,
To manage time and keep us fine.
They help us sort what must be done,
So we don't try to do each one.

Distractions fade when goals are set,
Priorities are clear, no need to fret.
A sense of accomplishment fills our day,
As each task completed clears the way.

We're not alone in this endeavor,
God's with us, now and forever.
In our weakness, His strength we find,
Guiding us with love so kind.

So set your goals, and start the quest,
With God beside you, give your best.
Each step you take, in faith you'll grow,
With goals and God, your life will glow.

THE MORE TIME YOU SPEND WITH JESUS…..THE MORE
YOU WILL RESEMBLE JESUS!

Tuesday, June 24, 2025

MORAL SOCIETIES LAST

Moral societies are the ones that last,
In integrity and honesty, their foundations cast.
Prosperity and virtue, hand in hand,
A truth well-proven, across the land.

Great societies are moral, strong,
In faith and honor, they belong.
Trust, truth, and law, their guiding star,
In harmony, they shine afar.

Blossoming where love and respect reside,
In unity and faith, they abide.
A common belief in Someone high,
Greater than themselves, reaching the sky.

History shows this clear and bright,
Moral strength leads to lasting might.
Those who doubt, have not seen,
The power of virtue, pure and keen.

So let us build with faith and trust,
In God and truth, we place our thrust.
For in these values, societies grow,
And in their light, prosperity flows.

DON'T CONDEMN SOMEONE JUST BECAUSE THEY SIN
DIFFERENTLY THAN YOU DO!

Wednesday, June 25, 2025

THE ENEMY WITHIN

Today's world, with open wounds laid bare,
Demands we confront polarization, everywhere.
Brothers and sisters, affected and torn,
Call for unity, and plead for a new dawn.

In seeking to be free from enemies without,
We must not feed the enemy within, it's doubt.
To imitate hatred, violence, and strife,
Is to become the very darkness in life.

We must confront the tyrants' cruel face,
Without adopting their brutal pace.
For feeding the hatred they bestow,
Is the surest way to follow their shadow.

The enemy within is ancient and sly,
It's fear that binds us, and makes us cry.
But in this fear, we find a thread,
A common ground where hope is spread.

Let us not imitate the tyrants' path,
But seek in love, to bridge the wrath.
For in unity, compassion, and grace,
We can find hope, in every place.

TODAY, ASK YOURSELF: "WHAT AM I TO DO NOW TO BE
WHAT GOD WANTS ME TO BE?"

LOOK UPON THE CROSS

In this world, our hearts divide,
No cure is found, no peace inside.
Hurt persists, divisions grow,
An embrace from beyond we need to know.

On the cross, a vision clear,
Jesus' death, an end to fear.
Arms stretched wide, a love profound,
In silence, healing can be found.

Naked, vulnerable, God and man,
Hangs in pain, a sacred plan.
No bitterness in suffering's place,
Just pure love and endless grace.

Hands pierced through, no anger shown,
In His gaze, true trust is known.
A reconciling embrace so real,
In His wounds, our hearts can heal.

Look upon the cross and see,
Love's answer to our agony.
In His sacrifice, we're not alone,
In that trust, our hope is sown.

GOD LOOKED AT THE CROSS, THEN LOOKED AT YOU AND
SAID, "YOU'RE WORTH IT!

SMALL THINGS

The world shouts, "Think big, dream high!"
And small things are lost as days go by.
Private lives seem small, so obscure,
Deemed unimportant, less secure.

The family stage, a tiny play,
Ignored by those who look away.
"Make your mark," the world demands,
"Great causes need your heart and hands."

Small acts of love, unnoticed, pass,
As fleeting as shadows on the grass.
Compliments, sacrifices too,
Are brushed aside in the grand view.

But God sees all, the small and grand,
Each mustard seed, each gentle hand.
For in the small, true care is shown,
In every kindness, love has grown.

Seasons turn, time marches fast,
And what remains from years long past,
A tiny act, of cruelty or grace,
In small things, we find God's embrace.

GOD'S LOVE IS SO EXTRAVAGANT AND SO
INEXPLICABLE THAT GOD LOVED US BEFORE WE WERE
AN "US!"

GOD CALLS US INWARD

In a world of noise, no silence is found,
Excitement reigns, in chaos bound.
Activity calls, stillness is denied,
In restless hearts, peace cannot hide.

We think the world has all we lack,
That others' lives are on the track.
Our lives feel small, too timid, weak,
We chase more thrills, more goals we seek.

If lonely, find a friend, they say,
If restless, do more things each day.
Desires fulfilled, yet peace unkept,
In outward quests, true calm is swept.

The world suggests more is the key,
To ease the inner agony.
Yet restlessness, though trivialized,
Is where our soul's true quest resides.

God calls us inward, deep and true,
Beyond the world's distracting view.
Eternal peace, an immortal call,
Is in quiet hearts, where we find it all.

EACH OF US IS A MASTERPIECE OF GOD'S CREATION!

Sunday, June 29, 2025

GOD'S LOVE IS CONSTANT

We comfort the world when hearts align,
With love that's pure, with love divine.
God sees our hearts with eyes so true,
Feels for us more than we ever do.

No fear in God of our free will,
He loves us deeply, deeper still.
When doors are closed, He opens wide,
A path ahead, a light inside.

Though we turn back, knowing best,
God's patience holds, we are blessed.
Empathizing with despair,
God's love is constant, always there.

In every pit that we create,
God descends, no time to wait.
Amongst our wounds, our guilt, our fears,
He breathes out peace, He dries our tears.

So trust in God, and life will show,
Despite the trials, love will grow.
Tell the world to live and dare,
For in the end, all will be fair.

KEEP GOD FIRST. CHASE YOUR DREAMS, AND
EVERYTHING WILL WORK OUT FOR YOU!

Monday, June 30, 2025

GRATITUDE CAN CHANGE OUR VIEW

Through wounds we see the world so grim,
In self-pity's grasp, our light grows dim.
Bitterness, jealousy, cloud our sight,
We miss the goodness in the night.

But gratitude can change our view,
See blessings in the morning dew.
Jealousy fades, appreciation grows,
In others' goodness, love now flows.

To live without love, a sorrow deep,
Unspoken words, a heavy keep.
Express affection, let it be shown,
In loving hearts, true joy is known.

Make friends with friends, embrace their worth,
In their smiles, find heaven here on earth.
Appreciation, love, contrition too,
These bonds of life, renew, renew.

Thank those who love you, let them see,
Tell those you love, "You mean the world to me."
In frequent words of love and grace,
Find light and warmth in every place.

GOD'S GRACE IS YOUR INNER STRENGTH!

EXPRESS YOUR FAITH

If you do not use your right arm,
Its power fades, its muscles disarm.
Exercise keeps it ever alive,
Just as with faith, in order to thrive.

Faith kept hidden will decay,
It must be used, as shown each day.
Like instruments that must be played,
Idle they lose the music made.

Use the faith you've got, make it strong,
Neglect it and you do it wrong.
Exercise it, let it grow,
In acts of love, let it show.

Help others, love, forgive with grace,
Integrity, in life, forever embrace.
Hold high values, ideals bright,
In these, your faith takes flight.

Going to church, a blessing true,
A gift that many never knew.
Express your faith, let it inspire,
For in small acts, faith grows higher.

INSIDE ME IS A WEAK HEART, BUT BEHIND IT, IS A VERY,
VERY STRONG GOD!

Wednesday, July 2, 2025

FREEDOM IS THE GREATEST GIFT

Freedom is the greatest gift,
But also one that we must lift.
A double-edged sword, sharp and true,
It can build or destroy what we pursue.

Our ancestors fought to break the chains,
Through blood and tears, they bore the pains.
But now the challenge lies with us,
To live with freedom, and earn its trust.

It's not enough to simply fight,
We must choose wisely what is right.
For freedom can both bless and curse,
Without our wisdom, it will make things worse.

Freedom is such a dangerous grace,
A gift that asks us to embrace,
Responsibility, bold and clear,
To guard what we hold so dear.

For forebearers fought for freedom's breath,
But we must preserve it beyond their death.
To wield it well, to choose with care,
And make sure justice fills the air.

WHEN GOD WANTS YOU TO GROW, GOD MAKES YOU
FEEL UNCOMFORTABLE!

Thursday, July 3, 2025

EVERY INCH OF THIS LAND IS BLESSED

Every inch of this land is blessed,
From sea to sea, from east to west.
Together, let us build and strive,
To keep democracy alive.

Justice, mercy, peace we seek,
For every soul, the strong and weak.
May empathy replace divide,
And let love's hand be our guide.

With power used to lift the poor,
Let kindness reign forevermore.
For all who hunger, for all who yearn,
May we invite them in, and learn.

For in each heart, God's image lives,
And to each soul, our love He gives.
If we bring grace, and peace increase,
Our land will shine, be a place of peace.

May we become a beacon bright,
A blessing shared, a guiding light.
With unity and justice near,
We'll spread God's love, far and clear.

IF YOU THINK YOU'RE TOO SMALL TO BE AN EFFECTIVE
CHRISTIAN, YOU'VE NEVER BEEN IN BED WITH A
MOSQUITO!

Friday, July 4, 2025

Fourth of July

THE FIREWORKS BLAZE

On this 4th of July, the fireworks blaze,
Yet shadows of doubt obscure the haze.
A nation divided, in struggle and fight,
Each voice clamoring in the dead of night.

Democracy teeters, on a fragile thread,
As freedom's promise is often misread.
Injustice and prejudice, like storms, rage,
Threatening to tear our history's page.

Yet in the midst of turmoil and fear,
There lies a hope, a vision clear.
A land where every soul is free,
Living in harmony, as we're meant to be.

Freedom's a gift, but a sword as well,
Its double edge, a story to tell.
It can uplift, or it can divide,
Depending on how it's applied.

On this 4th of July, let's pledge anew,
To the ideals that see us through.
A land of freedom, brave and true,
Where justice reigns for me and you.

YOU WILL NEVER BE FREE UNTIL YOU FREE YOURSELF
FROM THE PRISON OF YOUR FALSE THOUGHTS – GOD

YOU'RE SPECIAL

Many times in life, we fall, we fail,
Decisions weigh, and troubles trail.
We may feel worthless, our value lost,
But our true worth we cannot exhaust.

Dirty, clean, crumpled, or fine,
To those who love us, we still shine.
Our worth isn't in deeds or fame,
But in who we are, just the same.

You're special, never forget this truth,
A light within you since early youth.
God's love for you is always strong,
In His eyes, you truly belong.

Count your blessings, not your woes,
In gratitude, your spirit grows.
Embrace the love that's always there,
In every breath, in every prayer.

No matter what may come your way,
Your value stands, come what may.
You're precious in the eyes of love,
A cherished soul from up above.

IF GOD DIDN'T FORGIVE SINNERS…..HEAVEN WOULD BE
TOTALLY EMPTY!

Sunday, July 6, 2025

THE TEACHINGS OF CHRIST

A person or a nation always in strife,
Needs self-examining in their life.
Principles are worth fighting for, so true,
But constant quarrels we must subdue.

Destruction may not always be near,
Yet misery lingers, bringing us fear.
Love brings patience, peace in sight,
For happiness, is the highest light.

To sit alone, at odds each day,
Is a cruel, lonely, painful way.
Seek new methods, paths so bright,
For human joy, do follow the light.

The teachings of Christ, guide us through,
In love and peace, we find life anew.
Understanding hearts will thrive,
In His love, where we come alive.

So let us turn from an endless fight,
Embrace love's power, ever shining bright.
For in unity, we find our place,
In Christ's teachings, boundless grace.

DEAR JESUS, MAKE ALL THE BAD PEOPLE GOOD…..AND
MAKE ALL THE GOOD PEOPLE NICE!

Monday, July 7, 2025

A LIVELY SINNER

During his life, Jesus was no passive soul,
He stirred strong views, he made people whole.
Salt of the earth, with love He came,
Changing lives, ever igniting a flame.

He calls us not to sit and stay,
In a church, just praying, without dismay.
Bold and dynamic, He wants us to be,
Living our faith, setting other hearts free.

"Better to be a lively sinner," they say,
Than a dull saint who fades away.
A sinner can seek Confession's grace,
A dull saint takes up only space.

Jesus sees a dull saint as a paradox true,
In pews, in schools, in offices too.
He calls for passion, a vibrant heart,
In every role, we're to play our part.

So live with love, and spirit bright,
Let faith and action ever unite.
For in this life, with Jesus as guide,
Boldly in His love, we must abide.

BEFORE YOU TALK, LISTEN. BEFORE YOU REACT, THINK.
BEFORE YOU CRITICIZE, WAIT. BEFORE YOU PRAY,
FORGIVE. BEFORE YOU QUIT, TRY!

Tuesday, July 8, 2025

THE ALPHABET OF LIFE

When we come to celebrate, we bring
The alphabet of life, for each and every thing.
With hearts of warmth, love's gentle gleam,
Enthusiasm, songs, and our dance's dream.

If its tiredness and despair we know,
Then it's pain and boredom, the letters show.
Bring them forth, let them be spent,
Then celebrate, in each moment you're lent.

Offer all, both joy and strife,
Each letter tells a part of life.
God takes them all, each broken part,
And forms the words within your heart.

In every cheer, in every sigh,
He forms the script, both low and high.
Our lives, a book, with pages turned,
In God's great hands, all lessons are learned.

So bring your alphabet, your days,
In sorrow's hues or joyful rays.
Do celebrate, for in His hands,
God makes the words, God understands.

TURN YOUR GREATEST WORRIES INTO YOUR DEEPEST
PRAYERS!

Wednesday, July 9, 2025

LORD, I'M GRATEFUL

Lord, I'm grateful for the joy,
Of knowing You, my heart's employ.
For all the mountains You have moved,
In life, Your love is so deeply proved.

When I was down in deep despair,
Your hand, O Lord, was always there.
The worries grew, heartaches did soar,
Yet Your strength lifted me once more.

I've never moved a mountain tall,
For my faith, Lord, feels too small.
But You, my rock, my guiding light,
Move mountains with Your power and might.

As long as mountains fill my view,
I'll trust in You to see me through.
For in Your hands, I find my way,
No fear can darken my brightest day.

With faith in You, I'll stand so strong,
In Your embrace, where I belong.
Mountains will move, and I will see,
Your love is forever guiding me.

GOD WON'T BE HANDCUFFED BY YOUR FAILURES OR
UNLEASHED BY YOUR SUCCESSES!

Thursday, July 10, 2025

COMMITMENT'S CALL

The cheering stopped, the crowds did wane,
When Jesus spoke of His cross and pain.
He opened doors, He invited everyone in,
For Jesus spoke of sacrifice and sin.

The cheering ceased, the truth laid bare,
Commitment's call, only a few would care.
A cross to bear, a heavy load,
For others' sake, a love's true code.

In silence, many walked away,
Unwilling hearts, afraid to stay.
But those who stayed, found life anew,
In Christ's own love, forever true.

The cross, a bond, a sacred tie,
With Jesus near, we can't deny.
A relationship so deep and wide,
In His embrace, we can all abide.

So let us learn from those who stayed,
In love and faith, we are joyfully remade.
With Jesus' cross, we find our way,
In Him, all our fears and doubts allay.

GOD IS GOING TO SEND YOU SOMEONE WHO WILL
CONSISTENTLY REMIND YOU WHO GOD IS!

Friday, July 11, 2025

TO HEAR YOUR EULOGY

Ever wonder what it'd be like,
To hear your eulogy, the words they'd strike?
What would they say, how would they feel,
Would their emotions be deep and real?

Would friends be sad, with tearful eyes,
Or share your truths in sweet surprise?
Would secrets spill, unknown to you,
Revealing depths you never knew?

What would it be to hear their hearts,
The love and praise that each imparts?
Those words unsaid while you were here,
Now spoken clear, sincere, sincere.

Would you delight in heartfelt tones,
The intimate talk in whispered zones?
Hearing how much you truly meant,
In moments shared, in time well-spent.

To listen in on those deep chats,
About your life, your laughs, your spats,
Would bring a warmth, a tender grace,
A love unmasked in that sacred space.

GOD DID NOT CREATE YOU TO JUST "BLEND IN!"

WHEN DECISIONS CALL

Society presents us choices so wide,
Options that with time do abide.
What guides us when decisions call?
Do we seek advice, try to heed them all?

Do we consult with friends so near,
Or colleagues whom we hold so dear?
What place does God hold in our quest,
When making choices, and seeking the best?

Are our needs the sole concern,
Or do we let compassion burn?
Do we think of others' desires,
As Jesus taught, with a love that inspires?

His life showed suffering's embrace,
A path we sometimes too must face.
Do we choose the right, though it's tough,
Or shy away from trials, thinking it's enough?

In choices made, let love be known,
With faith in God, we're not alone.
For in His guidance, we can find,
The strength to choose, with heart and mind.

"NORMAL" ISN'T COMING BACK, BUT JESUS IS!

Sunday, July 13, 2025

JESUS OFTEN SAYS, "DO NOT FEAR"

Jesus often says, "Do not fear,"
"Let not your hearts be troubled here."
Though health and family cause concern,
Our fears are more than we should yearn.

So many fears are falsely spread,
By the many voices on TV we're fed.
The news plays on our deepest dread,
And keeps us worried, as we are misled.

We need to seek God's view on life,
To ease our hearts, to calm our strife.
Ask God to change our attitude,
So we can find a peaceful gratitude.

A new perspective, fresh and bright,
To see our lives in a different light.
Like birds that sing when storms are through,
We too can find so many songs anew.

With faith in God, we cast aside,
The fears that in our hearts reside.
Embrace the peace that He can bring,
And lift our voices, so let us sing.

GOOD TIMES, BAD TIMES, AND EVERYTHING IN BETWEEN
– GOD HAS NEVER LEFT MY SIDE!

Monday, July 14, 2025

JESUS, A CARPENTER

Jesus chose to be a carpenter fine,
Among fishermen, His skills did shine.
Not one of His friends shared this trade,
Yet in wood and faith, His path was laid.

The carpenter seeks wood to transform,
He ventures out, through sun and storm.
With hands and tools, he crafts with care,
Creating beauty beyond compare.

Like Jesus, who seeks each lost soul,
He goes where we are, to make us whole.
Not waiting for us to find our way,
He comes to us, both night and day.

The carpenter mends what's worn and torn,
Turning rough wood into beauty reborn.
He builds, not breaks, with loving hand,
Restoring strength to what was planned.

Jesus heals and transforms us all,
He lifts the lame, the blind who call.
From death to life, from sinner to saint,
In His love, we find no restraint.

BECAUSE OF JESUS CHRIST, OUR FAILURES DO NOT HAVE
TO DEFINE US, THEY CAN REFINE US!

LET RELIGION SHAPE OUR SIGHT

Religion's not just beliefs or prayers,
Nor rituals, nor lofty airs.
It's how we see the world around,
For in altered views, true peace is found.

You and I walk the same cold halls,
In hospitals where pain forever calls.
We see the facts, both you and I,
But our perceptions don't comply.

One sees a world of endless strife,
A bitter joke that mocks our life.
Another sees resilience, grace,
In every tear-streaked patient's face.

The suffering speaks of life's great worth,
Of every soul's inherent mirth.
For if life weren't so deeply good,
Why would its loss be understood?

So let religion shape our sight,
To see the world in a different light.
In every fact, let's find the grace,
To see God's love in every place.

ASK GOD, NOT GOOGLE!

Wednesday, July 16, 2025

OFFER A HAND

There is one way to look down right,
Offer a hand, lift up someone's plight.
If contempt is all we show,
Then no kindness will they know.

But look down to give a hand,
Help them up, help them to stand.
For those we lift, it's extraordinary,
Since in our hearts, their worth we carry.

When you gaze from up above,
Ask yourself if it's with love.
"Where's my hand?" should be your guide,
Is it hidden or opened wide?

In this way, true joy you'll find,
With a heart so warm and truly kind.
For helping others rise anew,
Brings happiness to me and you.

So look down, but with intent,
To give a hand, for a life's ascent.
In lifting others, we all grow,
In acts of love, let kindness show.

THE DESPERATELY POOR LEARN EARLY IN LIFE WHAT IT
TAKES MOST OF US A LIFETME TO LEARN…..WE'RE JUST
PASSING THROUGH!

WASTING TIME WITH OTHERS

We can learn to make the time,
To listen, share, in ways sublime.
Only then can love transform,
Changing us, helping us as we perform.

If we don't give our time away,
And spend it with others each day,
We'll waste it on things so hollow,
Leaving emptiness to follow.

In understanding, hearts are healed,
Experiences and love are revealed.
To change the world, we must first start,
By opening up, every heart to heart.

Wasting time with others shows,
The kind of love that deeply grows.
At day's end, it's time well-spent,
With connections, we're content.

So let us cherish moments shared,
In giving time, to show that we care.
For in this love, we find our way,
Changing the world, day by day.

SOME OF THE BEST THINGS GOD WILL DO IN YOUR LIFE
WON'T BE ON YOUR SCHEDULE!

Friday, July 18, 2025

LET GO OF THE PAST

To find peace of mind, let go of the past,
Bury grudges deep, let resentment be cast.
Suspicion breeds sorrow, unhappiness rife,
Let go of these burdens, embrace a calm life.

In dwelling on failures, depression takes hold,
Old mistakes, unwholesome, their stories retold.
Live in the present, let bygones be done,
In life's fleeting moments, find solace and fun.

Fight not with the world, accept and adapt,
Time's wasted where dreams have been trapped.
Cooperate with life, embrace what is real,
For running away brings no true appeal.

Stay in the world, be present and true,
Involvement in living, brings joy anew.
Resist reclusion, in stress do not hide,
Face challenges, let courage be your guide.

Indulge not in pity when life turns unfair,
For sorrow and trials are burdens we share.
Cultivate laughter, love, loyalty bright,
And find in compassion, a guiding light.

YOU HAVE A GOD WHO BELIEVES IN IMPOSSIBILITIES!

GOD IS THERE

We all are tempted, at times, to see,
If peeking at the future, how different it would be.
What lies ahead, what's around the bend?
God is there, our faithful friend.

His presence promised, ever near,
In every moment, year by year.
His grace sufficient, meets our need,
In every trial, God will always lead.

Our times and lives in God's hands rest,
With Him, we always are blessed.
No fear of the future, no need for dread,
With God's guidance, we are always led.

In trust and faith, we walk this land,
For every step, He's planned.
Around each corner, His love we find,
With grace and mercy, intertwined.

So let us live without the fear,
Knowing God is always here.
In His hands, our lives unfold,
In His presence, we are bold.

I TRUST THE NEXT CHAPTER OF MY LIFE BECAUSE I
KNOW THE AUTHOR!

Sunday, July 20, 2025

A PICTURE OF JESUS

A picture of Jesus hangs on our wall,
A symbol of love, admired by all.
But is He just a figure we see?
Or does He live in you and in me?

To truly know Him, we must take Him down,
Off the wall, from His holy crown.
Into our hearts, let Him reside,
Walking with us, side by side.

In daily life, let His love truly shine,
Not just in a picture, but in our hearts divine.
Embrace His teachings, feel His grace,
In every moment, and in every place.

How often do we let Him in,
Beyond the picture, beneath our skin?
To live with Him, day in, day out,
This is what faith is truly all about.

So take Him off the wall today,
Let His spirit guide your way.
In every breath, in every part,
Let Jesus dwell within your heart.

THE JESUS INSIDE ME IS STRONGER THAN THE
DARKNESS THAT THREATENS TO OVERTAKE ME!

"REMEMBER ME, MY CHILD!"

MONEY says: "Earn me, forget everything!"
In the chase for wealth, our hearts may cling.
TIME says: "Follow me, forget the rest!"
In the race of life, we forget what's best.

FUTURE says: "Struggle for me, forget today!"
In worry and fear, we lose our way.
GOD simply says: "Remember me, my child!"
In His love and grace, we are reconciled.

MONEY... TIME... FUTURE... they all demand,
Yet in God's hands, our lives are planned.
What are you missing, in this busy strife?
WHO are you forgetting, in your life?

Seek not the fleeting, but what is true,
In God's embrace, life starts anew.
Remember His promise, let go of the fray,
In His presence, find peace each day.

In the world's noise, hear His call,
For in His love, we find it all.
Let go of the worldly chase, and you'll see,
In God's remembrance, lies true harmony.

DEAR GOD, LET YOUR VOICE BECOME THE LOUDEST ONE
I HEAR AND THE ONE I'M MOST SENSITIVE TO.

A FLOURISHING TREE

Greatness may not be for all to claim,
But growth is ours, surely a steady flame.
Each day a chance to be more mature,
To strive to be better, to seek and endure.

When we forget this vital truth inside,
We lose life's meaning, its deepest guide.
Fulfillment fades, its source unknown,
In growth and change, our purpose is shown.

A seed underground, in dark confined,
Breaks through the soil, sunlight to find.
It's not content in its potential to stay,
It reaches higher, come what may.

So must we, in faith, not remain still,
But grow and stretch, seeking God's will.
In each moment, let our spirits ascend,
Towards the light, and around each bend.

For in this journey, we find our way,
Growing in grace, day by day.
Not just a seed, but a flourishing tree,
In God's garden, we're thriving and free.

SINCE GOD HOLDS THE UNIVERSE TOGETHER, GOD IS
HOLDING YOUR WORLD TOGETHER AS WELL!

TWO CATERPILLARS

Two caterpillars on the grass did crawl,
A butterfly above, soaring tall.
One nudged the other, with a laugh so bright,
"You couldn't get me in that for all my might!"

But what is God's dream for me and you?
To stay as we are, or for us to break through?
A caterpillar's life or butterfly's wings to try,
God has a wondrous plan for us to fly.

In every being, a purpose lies,
A destiny that's written in the skies.
For each creation, there's a reason true,
A path that God has eternally laid for you.

So doubt not the dream that God imparts,
For its etched deeply in our hearts.
From humble beginnings, we rise and soar,
To be more than we were before.

Embrace the journey, the purpose we find,
In God's design, our souls are aligned.
From a caterpillar's crawl to a butterfly's flight,
In His plan, we must always find our light.

GOD CHANGES CATERPILLARS INTO BUTTERFLIES, SAND
INTO PEARLS, AND COAL INTO DIAMONDS. USING TIME
AND PRESSURE, GOD'S WORKING ON YOU TOO!

Thursday, July 24, 2025

EMBRACE THE VALUES

We have taller buildings, but tempers so short,
Wider highways, but views of a narrow sort.
We spend more, but seem to have less,
We buy more things, but joy we suppress.

Bigger houses with families small,
More conveniences, yet time seems to crawl.
We've multiplied our possessions, yet values decline,
In our pursuit, we've left true worth behind.

We talk too much, but seldom love,
Hatred rises where peace is unheard of.
We've learned to make a living, but not a life,
Years we've added, but filled with strife.

Conquered the atom, yet prejudice remains,
We rush through life, but patience wanes.
These are our times, a paradox clear,
In all our progress, true meaning's not near.

Let's find balance, in love and grace,
To fill our years with a kinder pace.
Embrace the values that bring true cheer,
For in simple joys, life becomes clear.

THE BEAUTIFUL THING ABOUT GOD IS THAT EVEN
THOUGH WE CANNOT FULLY COMPREHEND GOD'S LOVE,
GOD FULLY COMPREHENDS US!

A JOURNEY FOR ALL TRUTH

All truth goes through three stages,
A journey through so many sages.
First, it's laughed at, scorned with glee,
A spectacle for everyone to see.

In its infancy, it's often mocked,
Chained by doubt, and even blocked.
Eyes roll and voices jeer,
Casting shadows, and spreading fear.

Second, truth faces a violent fight,
A battle in the darkest night.
Opposition fierce and loud,
Yet truth stands tall amid the crowd.

Third, truth dawns in the morning's light,
As soul after soul gains insight.
Once a whisper, now a song,
Truth echoing where it belongs.

Self-evident, the truth now stands,
In the hearts and in the hands
Of those who once refused to see,
But now are embracing what must be.

JUST BE WHO GOD MADE YOU TO BE!

Saturday, July 26, 2025

IN THE END LOVE TRIUMPHS

In the end, love triumphs over hatred's might,
Its gentle whisper conquers the darkest night.
Peace does triumph over chaos and strife,
Calming the storm, bringing harmony to life.

Forgiveness does triumph over bitterness deep,
Healing wounds, where shadows used to creep.
Hope does triumph over cynicism's snare,
Lighting the way, and dispelling despair.

Fidelity does triumph over despair's hold,
A steadfast promise, unwavering and bold.
Virtue does triumph over sin's dark sway,
Guiding us gently along the righteous way.

Conscience does triumph over callousness cold,
With compassion and empathy, stories unfold.
Life does triumph over death's cruel sting,
In the resurrection, new beginnings take wing.

In the end, it's God's love that prevails,
A divine promise that never fails.
The resurrection makes this point clear,
God has the last word, for God is ever near.

WE CAN MAKE OUR PLANS, BUT THE LORD DETERMINES
OUR STEPS!

Sunday, July 27, 2025

WHERE INTEGRITY IS ALWAYS FOUND

We suffer now from a lack of grace,
We expect the worst in every place.
In politics, business, faith, and art,
We've lost the trust that's in the heart.

Jesus taught us, life's not split,
Into compartments where we fit.
One way at home, another out,
This hypocrisy surely brings doubt.

The Pharisees, they acted thus,
Claiming God was part of us.
Yet their lives were far from true,
Their words a lie, their hearts askew.

For some proclaim, with the loudest voice,
That God has made them His own choice.
Though they live a life that's profane,
They say they're chosen in His name.

But we are called to a higher ground,
Where integrity is always found.
To stand for truth, to never bend,
To be honest to the very end.

REMEMBER: 1. GOD HEARS MY PRAYERS, 2. I AM NOT
ALONE, 3. MY VOICE IS VALUABLE, 4. I HAVE A
POWERFUL DESTINY, 5. NOTHING IS IMPOSSIBLE WITH
GOD!

TWO GIANTS AND A WORM

Upon two towering mountains high,
Two giants stood beneath the sky.
Each day they'd bellow, scream, and shout,
Their insults echoing all about.

"You're weak!" one giant roared in rage,
"Your mind's as dull as a broken blade!"
The other fired back with scorn,
"You're a fool since the day you were born!"

Their voices thundered, shook the ground,
Their bitter words, a mighty sound.
Yet down below in the valley green,
A humble worm could still be seen.

Amidst the clamor, fierce and loud,
The worm emerged, both small and proud.
It raised its head and smiled to say,
"Thank you, God, for such a beautiful day!"

The giants paused, their anger stalled,
A silence on the mountains called.
For in the worm's contented plea,
A truth was clear for all to see.

SUNRISES ARE HELLOS FROM GOD!

TREAT OTHERS KINDLY

How do you want your children to play,
On the playground where they spend their day?
Do you want them pushing, and starting a fight,
Using harsh words, displaying their might?

Do you want them thinking only of self,
Caring for no one else's health?
Or do you wish for them to show respect,
Polite and fair, with kindness reflect?

And how about adults in life's great game,
Should they be rude, harsh, and profane?
Caring for no one, just their own gain,
Adding to the world's burden and pain?

Or do you dream of a different scene,
Where respect and civility are keen,
Decency, courtesy, and openness thrive,
Making for a world where all can strive?

Let us teach both young and old alike,
To treat others kindly, to do what's right,
For in this world, big or small,
Respect and love can conquer all.

GOD SPECIALIZES IN GIVING PEOPLE A FRESH START!

Wednesday, July 30, 2025

THE RICH MAN STOOD

The rich man stood with fields so wide,
His barns were full, he burst with pride.
He pulled them down, built bigger ones still,
For crops and wealth, he had his fill.

"Eat, drink, be merry," the Lord did say,
"Tomorrow you die, no more to stay."
A failure masked by grand success,
A life of plenty, yet so much emptiness.

On a hill, a cross did stand,
With nails that pierced a gentle hand.
A crown of thorns upon His head,
A sight that filled the world with dread.

Yet in this scene of deep despair,
A victory bloomed beyond compare.
For in Christ's death, we are all reborn,
We have no reason to ever mourn.

The rich man's barns, now empty, stand,
A lesson learned in every land.
For wealth can fade and pride can fall,
But love and sacrifice transform it all.

YOU WERE MADE <u>BY</u> GOD AND <u>FOR</u> GOD. UNTIL YOU
UNDERSTAND THAT, YOUR LIFE WILL NEVER MAKE
SENSE!

A BOY PICKED A DAFFODIL

A boy picked a daffodil bud one day,
And studied its form in a curious way.
He tried to force it into bloom,
But limp petals fell, sealing its doom.

A mess of a flower, lifeless and dead,
Left the boy puzzled, scratching his head.
"How does God open it into a beautiful flower?"
He pondered aloud, in a reflective hour.

Then a light of understanding came,
"I know," he exclaimed, "God's not the same.
He works from within, gentle and slow,
Creating beauty in a steady flow."

For inside the bud, where eyes can't see,
God's greatest work unfolds naturally.
Each petal unfurls in perfect grace,
A masterpiece in its rightful place.

And so it is with the hearts of men,
God's finest work, again and again.
From deep within, God shapes and molds,
A story of love and our life unfolds.

GOD CAN MAKE GREATNESS OUT OF A GREAT MESS!

Friday, August 1, 2025

A HAND TO HOLD

A little boy and girl sat at an ocean site,
Built a castle in the sand, a sheer delight.
With gates and towers, a moat so wide,
No attention paid to the incoming tide.

Their masterpiece, nearly complete,
An elaborate work, right at their feet.
But then a wave, so vast and grand,
Came crashing down upon the sand.

The castle gone, just wet sand there,
No tears, no cries, and no despair.
Instead, they ran, laughing hand in hand,
Down the beach, all across the sand.

Laughter echoed, pure and free,
As they returned, filled with glee.
To build again, another castle new,
Their spirits high, their hearts were true.

For in life's journey, waves will come,
To wash away what we've begun.
But those who have a hand to hold,
Possess a treasure not made of gold.

DON'T MISS OUT ON A BLESSING TODAY BECAUSE IT IS
NOT PACKAGED THE WAY YOU WANT!

"TELL ME ABOUT GOD!"

There was a boy, with eyes so bright,
Who longed to see a wondrous sight.
His newborn sister, so soft and small,
His being alone with her, said it all.

His parents worried, and kept him near,
But he pleaded with many a tear.
One night they agreed, his wish came true,
So into her room alone, the little boy flew.

He leaned into her crib, so very close,
With tender words, he especially chose.
A whisper soft, a plea so mild,
To his sister, the newborn child:

"Tell me about God," he said,
"I'm starting to forget," he pled.
In her presence, pure and new,
He sought the truth he once knew.

For in her eyes, so fresh and bright,
He saw a glimpse of heaven's light.
A connection deep, a sacred call,
A reminder of the love that's in us all.

TALK TO GOD. GOD WANTS TO HEAR YOUR HEART!

Sunday, August 3, 2025

ASK THREE QUESTIONS

Ask three questions to see what's inside:
What makes you laugh, with nothing to hide?
What makes you angry, and ready to fight?
What makes you cry, long into the night?

Some say we need leaders filled with rage,
To fight the battles, to storm the stage.
But anger alone, though fierce and strong,
Can miss the mark, can steer us wrong.

We need anguish, a deeper plea,
A broken heart that yearns to see.
The difference clear, as night from day,
Is a heart that breaks, but finds its way.

Jesus, He showed us how to feel,
With righteous anger, a heart so real.
He cleansed the temple, fury bright,
Yet wept for the city, during the night.

So ask three questions, learn what's true,
Find the depth in those around you.
In laughter, anger, as well as in cries,
See a person's soul, through honest eyes.

GOD WILL MAKE YOU INTO WHAT YOU CANNOT MAKE
OF YOURSELF!

THE EAGLE OR THE OYSTER?

God created the oyster, secure and still,
In a shell that shelters, a haven at will.
A house to protect him from enemies near,
He just opens his shell, and food will appear..

God created the eagle, with skies so wide,
Unlimited space, where dreams reside.
He builds his nest on the highest peak,
Where storms threaten, fierce and bleak.

The oyster is freed from want, a life at ease,
A peaceful existence, beneath the seas.
For food, the eagle flies through wind and rain,
Facing the elements, ever bearing the strain.

Which life inspires you, and stirs your soul,
What dreams for your children, what is your goal?
The life of the oyster, safe and sound,
Or the flight of the eagle, ever unbound?

So ask yourself, and those you love,
What calls your spirit, what dreams rise above?
To live in comfort, or to dare and roam,
To find your place, and to make it your home.

JESUS LOVES YOU THE WAY YOU ARE, BUT TOO MUCH
TO LEAVE YOU THAT WAY!

LOOK BEYOND THE BARS

Two men looked out from prison bars,
One saw mud, the other saw stars.
It all depends on this basic sight,
How we perceive both day and night.

This vision I hold of life and me,
Shapes my world, my destiny.
What we see is what we get,
In this truth, our paths are set.

To grow and be more fully alive,
We must our vision reassess, and revive.
Redress its faults, its skewed display,
Eliminate distortions, and clear the way.

Real change, real growth, begins within,
When perception shifts, and we begin
To see with eyes unclouded, and clear,
The world as it truly does appear.

To see the world through God's own eyes,
Is to reach for truth, beyond the lies.
So look beyond the bars that confine,
Find the stars, and let your spirit shine.

JESUS LOVES YOU NO MATTER HOW MANY MISTAKES
YOU HAVE MADE!

Wednesday, August 6, 2025

THE GIFT OF TIME

Time is the raw material, deep and grand,
The inexplicable essence that's in our hand.
With it, all dreams can take their flight,
Without it, nothing seems to go right.

The supply of time, a daily grace,
A miracle each dawn that we face.
You wake, your wallet is filled anew,
With twenty-four hours, precious and true.

From these hours, twenty-four in all,
We spin our lives, both great and small.
Health and pleasure, wealth and cheer,
Contentment, respect, and growth sincere.

The evolution of our immortal soul,
Is woven in time, our ultimate goal.
We shall never have more time than this,
Each moment given, is a fleeting kiss.

We have, and always had, enough,
All the time there is, both smooth and rough.
So cherish the hours, let none slip by,
For in their passing, we live and we die.

WHEN IT'S NOT GOD'S TIME, YOU CAN'T FORCE IT. WHEN
IT'S GOD'S TIME, YOU CAN'T STOP IT!

Thursday, August 7, 2025

COUNTER-INTELLIGENCE

At a busy airport, travelers were in line,
Waiting for tickets, and passing the time.
Two boisterous women, with suitcases grand,
Elbowed their way ahead, and took their stand.

A man at the front, with wary eyes,
Saw the commotion, heard the sighs.
Fearing chaos might soon ensue,
He hatched a plan, simple and true.

With a gentle nod and humble grace,
He offered them his own cherished place.
Everyone watched, surprise in their eyes,
As silence descended from bustling skies.

The man took his bags, walked to the back,
An act of humility, no courage did he lack.
What could have been chaos, a brewing storm,
Turned in a moment, to a different norm.

In that airport, a lesson was taught,
Genuine kindness, a battle not fought.
Counter-intelligence, in the simplest deed,
Turned disaster to magic, where all hearts agreed.

THE WILL OF GOD CAN NEVER LEAD YOU TO WHERE THE
GRACE OF GOD CANNOT KEEP YOU!

Friday, August 8, 2025

THE AGE OF EFFICIENCY

We live in the age of efficiency,
We streamline each process meticulously.
Eliminating the waste of time,
In a quest for a life that's prime.

We have efficiently erased the past,
Where human interactions could last.
The future, bright with technology's gleam,
Heads forward toward an efficient dream.

We're in a time where we don't prize,
The warmth of a human's loving eyes.
We stare at screens both small and wide,
Ignoring the people right by our side.

Service, love, and tender care,
With sacrifice, now all seem rare.
Our culture is focused on the goal,
Of absolute efficiency, that has no soul.

So let us cherish our human touch,
The love, the care, that means so much.
For in the end, it's these we'll find,
That leave a lasting mark behind.

GOD CREATED YOU TO DO MORE THAN SPEND YOUR
WHOLE LIFE STARING AT A SCREEN!

Saturday, August 9, 2025

GOD DOES NOT COMPARE US

We grow up laden with grades and scores,
Statistics shape us, and close many doors.
We learn, early in our life, and it's true,
We must measure up, in all we say and do.

But in all this comparison, the joy of living flies,
Right past us, unnoticed, beneath the vast skies.
We're bent on comparing, on being the best,
Forgetting that in life, that love makes us blessed.

God does not compare us, nor rank us by our worth,
Each one is precious, a unique soul on earth.
Though I get this in my mind, intellectually clear,
On an emotional level, acceptance is not near.

For in a world that measures, ranks, and divides,
It's hard to feel good enough, to cast self-doubt aside.
But God's love is vast, beyond what we perceive,
In His eyes, we're cherished, no need to achieve.

So let's unlearn this habit, of constant compare,
And find joy in our journey, in moments so rare.
For in God's boundless love, there's no rank or race,
Just grace and acceptance, in His warm embrace.

WHEN YOU FULLY REALIZE THAT YOU MAY HAVE YOUR
BREAKFAST ON EARTH AND HAVE YOUR SUPPER IN
ETERNITY, TEMPTATIONS WILL LARGELY FALL AWAY!

Sunday, August 10, 2025

JESUS WANTS BOLDNESS

Jesus was no passive patsy, a shadow in the light,
He stirred strong opinions, igniting hearts in the night.
The salt of the earth, changing lives profound,
Wherever He walked, love and truth were found.

Jesus doesn't call us to be merely kind and good,
Church-goers who quietly stand where they should.
Jesus wants boldness, imagination, and fire,
Dynamic Christians who lift others higher.

In today's world, it's easy to blend,
To be tasteless and dull, no message to send.
But we are called to enrich every life,
To bring joy and light, and dispel the strife.

With an engaging manner, let our faith shine through,
In every action and word, let it be true.
So others may say, "He is so refreshing, so rare,"
"She is delightful, her faith beyond compare."

For in this spark, in the light we share,
We follow Christ's path, with love and care.
Bold, imaginative, dynamic, and bright,
We reflect His love, in the world's night.

JESUS DIDN'T COME TO TELL US THE ANSWERS TO THE
QUESTIONS OF LIFE. JESUS CAME TO BE THE ANSWER!

Monday, August 11, 2025

NEGLECT IS A POWERFUL WORD

Neglect. A powerful word, laden with weight,
So many family members suffer such a fate.
Neglect. Spouses neglected. Children neglected.
Older parents neglected. Responsibilities expected.

Opportunities neglected. It haunts all of life,
A shadow over joys, it's a source of strife.
Neglect. A neighborhood can be neglected.
A home, a garden, are left unprotected?

Neglect. What neglect is there to your dismay?
What corners of your heart have fallen in disarray?
For neglect is a silent thief, stealing joy and care,
Leaving emptiness and sorrow in its lonely lair.

We must shine a light on this shadowed place,
And tend to our hearts, with love and grace.
To nurture our relationships, our duties, our dreams,
To mend what's neglected, to stitch broken seams.

For in the tending, in the care we give,
We find the essence of what it means to live.
So let us not neglect, but cherish and hold,
All our precious gifts, more valuable than gold.

JESUS DIED FOR YOU, KNOWING THAT YOU MIGHT
NEVER LOVE HIM BACK. THAT IS TRUE LOVE!

CALLED TO BE COMPASSIONATE

We are called to be compassionate, and kind,
A divine spark of empathy, in each heart we find.
Compassion, born of God, is a sacred flame,
To enter another's struggles, is a whole new game.

It means stepping into another's sorrow,
Sharing their burdens, finding a hope for tomorrow.
Standing in their shoes, feeling their plight,
Transforming darkness into a new warm light.

In taking on their burdens, we show we care,
A bond of humanity, a love we share.
For in their trials, we see our own,
A shared journey, together we've grown.

Compassion is the way to humanize,
To look beyond, to see with loving eyes.
A heart that listens, a soul that understands,
Reaching out, with our own gentle hands.

To be compassionate is a divine call,
To lift others up whenever they fall.
In every act of kindness, love is shown,
In compassion's light, we are never alone.

BLESSED ARE THOSE WHO GIVE WITHOUT
REMEMBERING AND WHO TAKE WITHOUT FORGETTING!

Wednesday, August 13, 2025

GOD SEES EACH HEART

We feel a sense of insignificance, so profound,
Gazing at the starlit sky, the wonders astound.
In the vast expanse, we feel so very small,
Our planet is but a speck, in the cosmic hall.

Yet in this grand universe, vast and wide,
God sees each heart, since none can hide.
No matter how insignificant we seem to be,
God's love is boundless, embracing you and me.

Our heartache is known to the divine,
Every whisper of pain, every troubling sign.
Though the world may turn away, and pass us by,
God's attentive love hears our every cry.

In the darkest night, under stars that gleam,
We're held in God's most tender dream.
No sorrow too small, no tear unseen,
In God's eyes, we're cherished, serene.

So when you feel so small, lost in the vast expanse,
Remember God's love, as a divine dance.
For in the cosmic grandeur, one truth stands tall,
God's love enfolds us, one and all.

GOD SEES HEARTS THE WAY WE SEE FACES!

LIFE'S FLEETING SPAN

I went to the funeral of a man my own age,
We worked together, and we turned life's page.
He died suddenly, over a weekend's breath,
A stark reminder of life's swift, silent theft.

In only two weeks, he's already replaced,
His wife's moving away, her grief never erased.
Two weeks ago, he was fifty feet from me,
Now it's as if he never came to be.

Like a rock in water, ripples quickly fade,
The pool is calm, the rock's absence made.
I can't help but think, it could happen to me,
One day gone, and I'm hardly a memory.

I lie awake, pondering life's fleeting span,
Can any more meaning be found for a man.
Is a life any more than a brief, passing spark?
A light extinguished, that leaves only dark?

Our lives should be more, than just fading away,
Leaving a legacy, to be remembered, I pray.
For a man's life should echo, long after he's gone,
A testament of love, a spirit that lives on and on.

IF YOU WANT TO CHANGE YOUR RELATIONSHIP WITH
GOD, THEN CHANGE THE KIND OF QUESTIONS YOU ASK
GOD!

Friday, August 15, 2025

Mary's Assumption

MARY HEARS OUR PLEAS

Mary was taken, body and soul,
To heaven's glory, her perfect goal.
In God's embrace, she reigns as Queen,
Of heaven and earth, forever seen.

Though crowned above, she's not afar,
She's close to us, like a guiding star.
In God, who dwells within our hearts,
Mary shares in all He imparts.

On earth, her love was for just a few,
But now with God, she's near to you.
She knows our prayers, our hopes, our fears,
And listens to us through all the years.

Given to us by Christ, her Son,
A mother to all, to everyone.
With motherly kindness, she draws us near,
And offers her help when we are in fear.

In her, we trust our lives each day,
Mary hears our pleas when we pray.
Through her, we feel her Son's embrace,
For Mary reflects His boundless grace.

I'M ALWAYS HAPPY FOR PEOPLE WHEN I SEE GOD
BLESSING THEM THE WAY GOD HAS BLESSED ME!

Saturday, August 16, 2025

DEAR GOD, OPEN MY HEART AND MIND

Dear God, open my heart and mind,
To be fully present, gentle, and kind.
With all I meet and interact with today,
Guide my thoughts, show me your way.

Allow me to listen, clear and true,
Without passing judgement, without ado.
To hear each story, each voice, each plea,
With an open heart, let empathy be.

Let me not seek to solve or change,
What lies beyond my humble range.
Grant me patience, understanding deep,
In moments where troubles are steep.

Be with me in times of fatigue's embrace,
Fill me with strength, and Your loving grace.
Lift me up when my spirit is low,
Help me with Your light to glow.

Lord, grant me the courage to carry on,
Through each challenge, from dusk to dawn.
Let Your love flow through my deeds,
Tending to others' heartfelt needs.

EVERY TIME I COUNT MY BLESSINGS, MY LOVE FOR GOD
GROWS BIGGER. EVERY TIME I COUNT MY STRUGGLES,
MY FAITH IN GOD GROWS STRONGER!

Sunday, August 17, 2025

JESUS SAYS, "DO NOT BE AFRAID."

Fear startles us when the phone rings,
In the dead of night, the news it brings.
Our hearts race with a thousand fears,
For loved ones dear, we shed our tears.

We live in fear of what's to come,
Another pandemic that leaves us numb.
The unknown shadows loom so vast,
Haunting memories of the past.

The first words of Adam, stark and plain,
"I was afraid," he voiced his pain.
But Jesus spoke with a tender might,
"Do not be afraid," bringing us some light.

Through every fear, His voice is clear,
A balm to soothe, a love sincere.
"Do not be afraid," He gently said,
Calming storms, raising the dead.

So hold His words close to your heart,
"Do not be afraid," let fear depart.
For in His love, we find our way,
Through every night, to a brighter day.

FAITH IN GOD DOES NOT MAKE THINGS EASY. IT MAKES
THEM POSSIBLE!

Monday, August 18, 2025

WE HAVE LOST THE WONDER OF THINGS

We have lost the wonder of things,
Forgotten the magic that each day brings.
We live on a blue planet, vast and wide,
Circling a ball of fire, where miracles reside.

Next to a moon that moves the sea,
An endless dance of harmony.
How can you not believe in the divine,
In God's great work, so pure, so fine?

The stars that twinkle in the night,
The sun that rises, bringing light.
The earth that spins, the tides that sway,
All part of God's grand display.

The mountains tall, the rivers wide,
The beauty that we cannot hide.
The birds that sing, the flowers bloom,
In every breath, in every room.

How can we not see His miracles here,
In every moment, both far and near?
Open your eyes, let your heart be still,
Feel God's presence, know His will.

IT'S MONDAY! I'M BREATHING. I'M ALIVE. I'M BLESSED.
I'M HUMBLE. I'M THANKFUL. GOD IS GREAT!

Tuesday, August 19, 2025

GOD IS UP TO SOMETHING

Uncertainty has a way of creeping in,
Just when life seems calm, we begin again.
Everything's under control, plans set in stone,
Then a storm arises, and we're left alone.

A pandemic strikes, or trials unfold,
Shaking foundations, making us feel cold.
In the chaos, we're left to ponder,
What went wrong, as we sit and wonder.

When you are down to nothing, feeling small,
Remember, dear heart, God is above it all.
In the depths of despair, when hope seems faint,
His love endures, a truth so quaint.

God is up to something, unseen and grand,
Holding us gently in His mighty hand.
"Fear not, my child, I am here,
In every struggle, in every tear."

When life unravels, and dreams fade away,
Trust in God's plan, come what may.
So hold on tight, through the stormy weather,
For God is up to something, now and forever.

GOD LOVES BROKEN PEOPLE, BECAUSE BROKEN PEOPLE
ARE ALL THAT THERE ARE!

Wednesday, August 20, 2025

DEAR GOD, HELP ME TO SEE

Dear God, help me today to see,
To focus on what truly matters to me.
Sometimes my mind is everywhere,
Lost in thoughts, floating in air.

Thank you for the many ways,
You center me through all my days.
Bringing me back to life anew,
Grounding me in love so true.

In moments when my mind does stray,
Pull me back, show me the way.
To see the light, to feel Your peace,
In Your presence, worries cease.

Help me cherish what is real,
In every thought, in all I feel.
To find in You as my solid ground,
Where love and purpose both are found.

Thank you, God, for being near,
For quieting every doubt and fear.
May my heart be firm and true,
Focused solely, Lord, on You.

NEVER LOSE HOPE. JUST WHEN YOU THINK IT'S
OVER.....GOD SENDS YOU ANOTHER MIRACLE!

Thursday, August 21, 2025

WHAT IS A FRIEND?

What is a friend? A treasure rare,
A soul with whom your heart you share.
Friends are those who let you be,
Your truest self, unbound, and free.

With them, no need to guard your heart,
They take you in, your every part.
They don't misjudge, they understand,
With a gentle voice and a steady hand.

With friends, you breathe a lighter air,
A space where you can simply care.
You weep, you sing, you laugh, you pray,
In their presence, worries go away.

Through all the storms, the joys, the strife,
They stand beside you, your whole life.
Their love is constant, deep, and true,
In every moment, they're with you.

So cherish friends, those hearts of gold,
In their embrace, let your stories be told.
For in their love, you find yourself,
A bond that's truly worth the world's wealth.

GOD MADE HUMAN BEINGS BECAUSE GOD LOVES
STORIES!

Friday, August 22, 2025

TO SAY "I'M SORRY" TAKES A HEART

It isn't easy to apologize,
To face your faults, to recognize.
But in that act, a strength is shown,
A sense of self, that's fully grown.

To say "I'm sorry" takes a heart,
That values truth, a humble start.
It means you cherish the bonds you share,
More than the pride you might declare.

Apologies mend bridges burned,
Show lessons learned, respect earned.
They speak of love that's deeply true,
A willingness to start anew.

So when you find you've gone astray,
Have courage, let your heart convey,
The words that heal, the steps that bind,
A humble, gracious peace of mind.

For in the act of making right,
You shine with a forgiving light.
To apologize is to reveal,
A soul that loves, and a heart that's real.

MOST CHRISTIANS ARE BEING CRUCIFIED TODAY
BETWEEN TWO THIEVES: YESTERDAY'S REGRET AND
TOMORROW'S WORRIES!

A GOOD APOLOGY

A good apology, sincere and true,
Has three parts to see it through.
First, "I'm sorry," heartfelt and clear,
Acknowledging pain, drawing us near.

Second, "It's my fault," a humble claim,
Owning the action, taking the blame.
Responsibility taken, no shifting of weight,
Honoring the truth, setting it straight.

Third, "What can I do to make it right?"
Most people forget this, losing sight.
It's the bridge to healing, the path to mend,
Showing a commitment, to the very end.

An apology isn't just words to say,
But actions taken to light the way.
To repair, to restore, to make amends,
To heal the hurt, to be true friends.

So remember these parts, keep them close,
In every apology, let them be your prose.
For in the third, true change is found,
In those words, new bonds are bound.

YOUR GIFT TO GOD IS HONESTY. GIVE IT! GOD'S GIFT TO
YOU IS THE TRUTH. TAKE IT!

"I DID IT FOR LOVE."

"I did it for love," five words so strong,
The driving force that moves us along.
The horsepower behind every good deed,
The reason we help, the reason we lead.

In everything worthwhile we pursue,
Love is the essence, pure and true.
Jesus tells us, "As I have loved you,
So you should love one another too."

His words a beacon, shining bright,
Guiding us through the darkest night.
In acts of kindness, great and small,
Love is the answer, the call for all.

For love compels us, hand in hand,
To build together, to understand.
In every smile, in every touch,
Love drives us forward, it means so much.

"I did it for love," let that be,
The motto of our legacy.
For in His love, we find our way,
To live with purpose every day.

WHEN THE EYES OF THE SOUL LOOKING OUT MEET THE
EYES OF GOD LOOKING IN, HEAVEN HAS BEGUN HERE ON
EARTH!

OLD AGE, A REWARDING TIME

Old age can be a most rewarding time,
Where life's sweet music turns to rhyme.
The birds sing sweeter, with clearer tune,
The winds blow softer, beneath the moon.

The sun shines more radiantly bright,
Casting a warm, even golden light.
My "outward person" may slowly fade,
But my "inward person" is joyously made.

As the years begin to show,
A deeper strength and beauty grow.
The essence shifts from form to soul,
A spiritual strength that makes us whole.

One is temporary, fleeting fast,
The other is forever and meant to last.
God planned this journey, every part,
To lead us gently, from heart to heart.

So embrace the twilight's gentle hue,
For in its glow, God's love shines through.
The strength of youth may pass away,
But the spirit's beauty will always stay.

THANK GOD TODAY FOR SIMPLE THINGS, LIKE BEING
ALIVE!

YOUR PRECIOUS FAITH IN WORDS

We pass our faith to our young ones dear,
In ways personal, sincere, and clear.
It's what our life with Jesus means,
In whispered prayers and quiet scenes.

Preaching to them often falls away,
Even good examples may not stay.
But put your precious faith in words,
Let them feel the love that stirs.

Share with them how you talk to Him,
In moments bright and shadows dim.
Tell them what you say in prayer,
How Jesus listens, and is always there.

Friends may come and friends may go,
But Jesus stays, this they must know.
He holds our hearts through joy and strife,
A constant presence in our life.

So speak of Him with honest grace,
They will see the light upon your face.
Let your words be soft and true,
Reflecting the faith that lives in you.

THE MEANING OF YOUR LIFE IS TO FIND YOUR GIFT
FROM GOD. THE PURPOSE OF YOUR LIFE IS TO GIVE
YOUR GIFT AWAY!

Wednesday, August 27, 2025

GOD'S MESSAGE IS CONSTANT

Since time began, God's voice has called,
A whisper in the wind, a thunder enthralled.
To draw our hearts to principles true,
To values deep and sacred, too.

God asks us to commit our days,
To live in love, in righteous ways.
A sense of sacredness in every breath,
A guiding light and a moral depth.

Sometimes we listen, hearts open wide,
Responding to God, walking beside.
Sometimes we ignore, lost in our plight,
Turning away from the divine light.

But God keeps trying, ever patient and kind,
With every sunrise, a gentle remind.
God works at getting our attention still,
Hoping we'll in time embrace His will.

He calls in the laughter, in the tears we shed,
In the love we share, in the paths we tread.
God's message is constant, unwavering, clear,
"Live with purpose, for I am near."

SEEK TO FIND GOD IN ALL THE CLUTTER OF TODAY!

WE ARE MIRACLES

Most people spend more time, it seems,
Defending beliefs, chasing after dreams,
Than seeking truth, in silence deep,
Where wisdom waits, where answers sleep.

We talk and plan our earthly days,
In countless, often fleeting ways.
But why not talk and plan the end,
Our eternity, where paths transcend?

Each heartbeat, each breath we take,
Is a wondrous gift, for heaven's sake.
We're here because, in every breath,
We ARE miracles, defying death.

So let us seek the deeper things,
Beyond the rush of worldly flings.
For in the grand design of all,
We ARE miracles, standing tall.

So ponder not just your earthly fight,
But the endless day, the eternal light.
For we ARE miracles, you and me,
Living in the now, and destined for eternity.

JESUS DIDN'T ONLY COME TO MAKE BAD PEOPLE GOOD.
JESUS CAME TO MAKE DEAD PEOPLE ALIVE!

Friday, August 29, 2025

A CHILD OF GOD

We need to look into a mirror clear,
And not just see, but hold it dear,
The reflection staring back at me,
Is a child of God, so wondrously free.

We must believe in the worth we hold,
A sacred story yet to be told.
With another's care, a guiding hand,
We find the strength to firmly stand.

We stare at screens for facts to glean,
Yet miss the truth that lies unseen.
For transformation's deeper call,
We must look beyond the digital wall.

To love another, heart and soul,
Is to glimpse the divine, to become whole.
In every kind and gentle face,
We find a touch of God's own grace.

Look in the mirror, see it's true,
The child of God residing in you.
Believe in yourself, and let it be known,
Through love and care, our souls have grown.

AT THE END OF THE DAY, YOU CAN FOCUS ON WHAT'S
TEARING YOU APART, OR WHAT'S HOLDING YOU
TOGETHER!

Saturday, August 30, 2025

BLESSED INTERRUPTIONS

So often we claim, with a hurried sigh,
"I don't have the time," as moments fly by.
Others infringe on what we pursue,
We rush through the day, with so much to do.

"I couldn't get a thing done today,"
We grumble and fret, in our own busy way.
But what is truly important, do we see?
It often happens in interruptions, unexpectedly.

Pray that God will open our eyes,
To see the needs that often arise.
Open our ears to hear the call,
Our hands to catch, when others fall.

Open our hearts to interruptions blessed,
Where healing and love are manifest.
For God provides, in moments unplanned,
So many opportunities to lend a hand.

So embrace the interruptions, kind and true,
For in them, God's love shines through.
In every moment, small or grand,
We find our purpose, and His guiding hand.

COUNTING YOUR BLESSINGS IS BETTER THAN RE-
COUNTING YOUR PROBLEMS!

Sunday, August 31, 2025

JESUS GAVE US THE EUCHARIST

For most of His ministry, Jesus spoke,
Using words to console, challenge, and evoke.
Through words, He brought God's strength and care,
Stirring hearts, healing wounds laid bare.

His words held power, profound and true,
They moved mountains, and brought light anew.
Yet in time, even words fell short,
For a deeper love, He had to resort.

On the night before He faced the cross,
Knowing words alone might be lost,
Jesus went beyond what words convey,
He gave us the Eucharist in a profound way.

A physical embrace, a divine kiss,
A sacred meal, a moment of bliss.
No longer just words, but presence real,
His love, His grace, in bread and wine we feel.

For when words alone could do no more,
Jesus gave us a gift to the core.
A meal of love, a holy sign,
Binding us forever, to the divine.

WHAT WE NEED IS JESUS, NOT WHATEVER QUICK FIX
WE'RE LOOKING FOR!

Monday, September 1, 2025

Labor Day

WORK CAN HONOR GOD

We often think God's glory appears
Only in worship, prayers, and tears.
But in our work, both great and small,
God's glory shines through it all.

Whether you cook or lead a team,
Build a future or chase a dream,
Slinging hash or corporate goals,
Each task can glorify our souls.

Digging dirt or patient care,
Every job becomes a prayer.
Serving food or fixing hearts,
God's grace is present in all the parts.

Pumping oil or pumping gas,
Every task we do can pass
As work that honors God above,
When done with purpose and with love.

So no matter what your hands may do,
In every job, God's glory's true.
With the right heart and attitude,
God is honored, with certitude.

SOMETIMES LIFE HAS THE TENDENCY TO WIPE AWAY A
SMILE. GOD HAS A TENDENCY TO KEEP YOU SMILING.

Tuesday, September 2, 2025

GOD KEEPS COMING BACK AGAIN

At each and every stage of life,
God reaches out through joy and strife.
Sometimes we're too preoccupied,
With school, job, and family by our side.

Yet God persists, with gentle grace,
Returning to each time and place.
In every moment, in every phase,
God seeks our hearts, through all our days.

The smile I wear, though life's not perfect,
Reflects all my blessings, that I collect.
Appreciation for what I hold dear,
God's love and presence is always near.

Through ups and downs, His touch remains,
In every joy, in all life's pains.
So let us pause and see God's hand,
Guiding us through life's wondrous land.

For God keeps coming back again,
Through all the stages, through loss and gain.
He calls to us with endless love,
A constant presence from above.

GOD IS NOT A CELESTIAL PRISON WARDEN JANGLING
KEYS. GOD IS A SHEPHERD LOOK FOR SHEEP. A FATHER
WAITING FOR HIS SON'S RETURN!

Wednesday, September 3, 2025

REALITY STANDS, FIRM AND CLEAR

The world exists on its own, apart,
Separate from our minds and heart.
Regardless of the beliefs we hold,
Its truths unfold, both brave and bold.

The climate warms, or it does not,
Belief alone won't change its plot.
Reality stands, firm and clear,
Whether or not we choose to adhere.

Our beliefs do matter, that is true,
For they shape the actions we pursue.
Align your mind with reality's sights,
Or poor choices will lead to fights.

I may not believe in gravity's pull,
But off the balcony, the result is full.
I'll hit the ground, just like the rest,
For reality's rules stand the test.

It's not reality that's in danger, you see,
But our own selves, if we don't agree.
So seek the truth, in every part,
And let wisdom guide your heart.

BE AS QUICK TO KNEEL AS YOU ARE TO TEXT!

Thursday, September 4, 2025

JESUS WAS NOT A POLITICIAN

Jesus was not a politician, we know,
In any sense of the word, the Gospels show.
He never pleaded ignorance's guise,
He always told the truth, without disguise.

No matter the consequences He faced,
His words were honest, never displaced.
Two thousand years, His challenge remains,
To speak the truth, despite the pains.

He calls on us, each soul, each heart,
To not plead ignorance, but to do our part.
To tell the truth, the whole truth and real,
No matter the wounds, no matter the deal.

Jesus showed us the righteous way,
To live in truth, come what may.
So heed His call, stand firm, be brave,
In every moment, in every wave.

Not a politician, but a truth divine,
Jesus' words, will forever shine.
To tell the truth, with courage bold,
Is to walk the path of His truth, retold.

THE MORE YOU STUDY THE LIFE OF JESUS, THE MORE
YOU WILL BE IMPRESSED WITH HIS ABSOLUTE, GENUINE
LOVE FOR ALL OTHERS.

PRAYING HANDS ARE BEGGING HANDS

Praying hands are begging hands,
Soft and open, like desert sands.
They are nonviolent, pure, and meek,
Showing the strength of those who seek.

In their clasp, vulnerability shines,
Proof of a heart that deeply pines.
For in this gesture, we cannot fight,
But show our need, in humble light.

I find that beautiful, useful too,
A symbol of faith, steadfast and true.
Putting hands together requires not much,
Not a sinless soul, just a gentle touch.

Putting my hands together, I set aside,
All distractions, all foolish pride.
In the cavity of my chest, I hear,
A hope that God is dwelling near.

Praying hands, so simple, yet profound,
In their silence, God's voice is found.
They show a soul, open and true,
Reaching for God, in all we do.

GOD OFTEN USES YOUR DEEPEST PAIN AS THE
LAUNCHING PAD FOR YOUR GREATEST CALLING!

Saturday, September 6, 2025

THE GAZELLE AND THE LION

Every morning in Africa, a gazelle awakes,
Knowing it must run faster than the lion stakes.
For if it doesn't outpace the fastest beast,
It will be killed, becoming the lion's feast.

Every morning, the lion wakes in the plain,
Knowing it must outrun the slowest gazelle again.
For if it doesn't catch its meal,
It will starve, that's the predator's deal.

It doesn't matter, lion or gazelle,
When the sun rises, in the wild, all's well.
When your feet hit the floor each day,
What motivates you to run, come what may?

Is it fear that pushes you ahead,
Or a sense of Mission in your head?
This question holds the key to life,
To rise above, to handle daily strife.

What Mission has God set for you,
When morning light turns dark to blue?
Has the news of the world made you shy,
Or do you find the courage to reach for the sky?

YOU NEED TO RELEASE THE LOAD GOD NEVER MEANT
FOR YOU TO CARRY, AND FOCUS ON WHAT GOD CALLED
YOU TO DO!

EUCHARIST AS FRESH BREAD

I believe in Eucharist as fresh bread,
A daily need, by Jesus we are fed.
You and I, we need this grace,
To nourish our souls, to find our place.

Every day, we must be aware,
Of hungry souls in need of care.
Not just on screens, both big and small,
But in the Bread of Life, we find our call.

Listen to the hunger deep inside,
A yearning that we cannot hide.
For every day, our souls do crave,
The fresh bread only Jesus gave.

We cannot fixate on digital gleam,
And forget the source of every dream.
Our souls need more than worldly fare,
They ned more love and constant care.

So come to the table, come and dine,
On the Bread of Life, the gift divine.
For in each bite, in every prayer,
We find the strength to love and share.

JESUS IS THE ONLY ONE WHO CAN LOVE EVERYTHING
YOU ARE DESPITE EVERYTHING YOU'RE NOT!

Monday, September 8, 2025

WE DRAW THE CIRCLE TOO SMALL

"What's the biggest problem today?"
Mother Teresa answered in her humble way.
"The biggest problem in the world that we see,
Is our circle of family is drawn too narrowly."

With all that's evil in our world today,
One could list countless wrongs on display.
That's what makes her response so profound,
A call to expand, to have love unbound.

She says the problem is not the world's state,
But how we see others, and how we relate.
We must see more people as family, so near,
Embrace them with love, dispel our every fear.

We draw the circle too small, too tight,
Excluding those who truly need our light.
For in loving others as we do ourselves,
We heal the world, as Mother Teresa tells.

Let's draw our circle wide and free,
Encompass all with empathy.
For the biggest problem that we face,
Is a lack of love, a need for grace.

THE LOVE OF JESUS ALWAYS HELPS YOU TO SEE
BEYOND THE FAULTS OF OTHERS!

THE CAUSE OF POLARIZATION

You are the cause of polarization, and I am too,
Together, we create this rift, it's true.
Unless we admit this, and take our share,
The situation worsens, a burden to bear.

Polarization isn't what just happens to us,
It's a divide we create, it's a growing fuss.
The temptation to think it's others to blame,
Is precisely the essence of this damaging game.

We must see our role in the widening breach,
In every action, every word we preach.
For it's not just them, but also you and me,
Creating this chasm, that's deep as the sea.

To heal this split, we must start within,
Admit our part in this collective sin.
Only then can we hope to truly mend,
The fractures between us, bring them to an end.

So let's confront this truth, and face it clear,
Acknowledge our role, and shed the fear.
For in unity, understanding, and grace,
We can find a path to a better place.

YOUR MIND WILL ALWAYS BELIEVE WHAT YOU FEED IT.
FEED IT FAITH. FEED IT TRUTH. FEED IT WITH LOVE!

I WISH I WAS A LITTLE KID OF TEN

I wish I was a little kid of ten
With someone to take care of me again.
Someone to clean up all my messes,
To guide me through life's tangled presses.

I want someone to remind me what's right,
To steer me clear, to keep me in sight.
To yell at me before I fall,
To watch my steps, to heed my call.

I want to be held in loving arms,
Shielded from life's harsh alarms.
To cry my heart out, free from fear,
In someone's embrace, warm and near.

But now I stand, grown and tall,
Facing the world, through it all.
Yet in my heart, the child remains,
Seeking comfort in life's gains and pains.

So while I walk this path alone,
I carry those wishes, deeply sown.
For the child within, still seeks the care,
Of a loving heart, that is always there.

GOD DOESN'T LOVE A "PAST" VERSION OF YOU OR A
"FUTURE" VERSION OF YOU, GOD LOVES YOU TODAY!

SEPTEMBER 11th

On September 11th, we were shown,
That we are not invincible alone.
To live in joy, in peace, and grace,
We must trust something beyond this place.

Our safety is not ours to keep,
We can't ensure it while we sleep.
So, we turn to God, to prayer and light,
To find our way through the darkest night.

An attack on all, on what is good,
Is a challenge to our brotherhood.
But we must answer with a hand,
That holds on to love and makes a stand.

Violence only leads to pain,
And vengeance fuels a bloody chain.
We must find justice, pure and true,
Not stoop to what the wicked do.

A world where hate is left to reign,
Is one where none are free from pain.
So we must fight for what is right,
With open hearts and clear-sighted might.

THE LIGHT OF GOD'S LOVE WILL PIERCE EVEN THE
DARKEST NIGHT!

Friday, September 12, 2025

WHAT IF GOD DECIDED TO TURN AWAY?

What if God couldn't take the time,
To bless us today, in rhythm and rhyme,
Because we didn't take a moment,
To thank Him yesterday, for all His love meant?

What if God decided to turn away,
To stop leading us into tomorrow's day,
Because we didn't follow His path so bright,
Ignoring His guidance, lost in our own flight?

What if God wouldn't hear our plea,
Today in our need, our desperate decree,
Because yesterday we closed our ears,
To His whispers, to His call, to His cheers?

Yet God's love, so vast, so pure,
Gives us chances, forever sure.
So let us heed and humbly strive,
To thank, to follow, to come alive.

For His blessings flow, unearned, so grand,
Guiding us with God's ever gentle hand.
May we respond with hearts sincere,
To serve, to listen, to hold Him near.

THANK YOU, GOD, FOR PUTTING PERIODS ON SENTENCES
THAT I WASN'T STRONG ENOUGH TO END!

CARRY KINDNESS WITH YOU

No matter where you go today,
Carry kindness with you, come what may.
A simple smile, so small and bright,
Can change a day from dark to light.

To pet a lonely dog or cat,
Shows your love and care, just like that.
A gentle touch, a caring hand,
Speaks volumes about where you stand.

Rise above all the hate and fear,
Let compassion guide you, it's crystal clear.
Live today with joy and grace,
In every heart, in every place.

For kindness is a gift we give,
A way to show how we truly live.
In every smile, in every deed,
We plant a loving, hopeful seed.

So carry kindness, let it flow,
To all you meet, let your goodness grow.
In simple acts, in gentle ways,
We find the beauty within our days.

GOD IS GOOD ALL THE TIME. GOD'S LOVE ENDURES
FOREVER. THE BEST IS YET TO COME. GOD'S PLANS
NEVER FAIL!

Sunday, September 14, 2025

JESUS' EXAMPLE

The world can teach a leader skills, it's true,
But only Jesus can teach a heart that's new.
His leadership, built on empathy, that's smart,
Shows us how to lead with a servant's heart.

"Whoever among you wants to lead, must serve,"
Said Jesus, with words that took a lot of nerve.
He didn't come to tell us about life's vast array,
He came to BE the answer, showing us the way.

To be a leader, one needs humility's grace,
Clarity in vision, courage in life's long race.
A leader translates a vision into reality,
Guiding others with truth and clarity.

A leader knows the way, and walks it true,
Shows the way, guiding us by all they do.
With Jesus' example, so bright and clear,
We find the path, and we hold it dear.

For in His teachings, of love and grace,
We find the strength to assume our place.
To lead with our heart, to serve and guide,
With Jesus' words to help us deep inside.

JESUS' LOVE BLAZES FORTH AND SCORCHES ALL
BITTERNESS, RAGE, ENVY, CONTEMPT, SHAME, AND
FEAR. IT CASTS OUT OUR EMOTIONAL TURMOIL!

Monday, September 15, 2025

LET'S RECLAIM THAT CHILDLIKE GRACE

Not too long ago, we were all children fair,
With hearts full of wonder, without a care.
Faith unwavering, joy so pure,
In a world of miracles, we felt secure.

For children, laughter is their song,
They play and dance all day long.
Each moment brims with anticipation,
A world alive with fascination.

Now as adults, we think we've changed,
Our attitudes and views are rearranged.
But the wonder and mystery still reside,
If only we'd let our hearts be our guide.

The miracles haven't gone away,
They're here with us, every day.
So let's reclaim that childlike grace,
And see the world with a smiling face.

The wonder, the magic, they still bloom,
In every heart, in every room.
Nothing's changed but how we see,
The world's still full of mystery.

WRAP YOURSELF IN GOD'S LOVE ON A DAILY BASIS AND
LET IT BE YOUR GUIDE FOR EVERYTHING YOU DO!

STEP OUT FROM BEHIND THE SCREEN

We must come back to contact with reality,
Move from the virtual to actuality.
From abstract thoughts to concrete ground,
Move from the adjective to the noun.

We've been lost in our own concerns,
Missing the world as it turns.
So focused on the "I" and "me,"
We've forgotten the "we" and "thee."

Let us step out from behind the screen,
Embrace the world, the sights unseen.
For in reality, in truth's embrace,
We find our hearts, our rightful place.

Move from the distant, the abstract thought,
To the concrete love that Jesus taught.
For in this journey, in this return,
A deeper wisdom we all will learn.

To see the faces, to hear the names,
To feel their joys, to share their pains.
For in this contact, life is found,
A sacred, holy, human ground.

WHEN BROTHERS AND SISTERS LOVE GOD FIRST, THEY
LOVE EACH OTHER BETTER!

THE MAIN EVENT IS HERE AND NOW

Jesus says we cannot serve both God and gold,
For greed destroys stories, both new and old.
The only thing that truly matters in the end,
Are your relationships with family and friend.

No corporate title, no wealth or gain,
Can replace the moments, simple and plain.
When a child or grandchild lays their head,
On your chest, as you lay on a peaceful bed.

Time spent with children, family, and friends,
Is not a distraction, but where love transcends.
It is the Main Event, the heart's true call,
The moments that matter, the greatest of all.

Greed may tempt with hollow dreams,
But love and time are the golden streams.
No trophy or title can compare,
To the love we give, the moments we share.

Serve not riches, but a love divine,
In every heart, let kindness shine.
For the Main Event is here and now,
In love's true presence, we humbly bow.

WHAT A BEAUTIFUL THING IT IS TO KNOW THAT JESUS'
LOVE FOR US IS SO GREAT THAT IT HAS ABSOLUTELY NO
WAY OF BEING MEASURED!

Thursday, September 18, 2025

I LIKE THE NEW ME

I like the new me, who weeps with delight,
To see the neighbor girl ride her bright pink bike.
A healthy child in motion, pure and free,
Such a beautiful sight, it moves me deeply.

I like the me who talks to trees,
Praising them for their grace and leaves.
"You're doing so well," I softly say,
"You look so good, in every way."

To see the world with open eyes,
To feel the wonder, to recognize.
That life is full of simple grace,
In every smile, in every place.

I like the me who finds delight,
In the smallest things, morning to night.
For in these moments, I have found,
A deeper peace, a joy profound.

So here's to the me who loves anew,
Who cherishes life, in all I do.
For life is bright, a canvas wide,
With love and wonder by my side.

LIFE IS TOO SHORT, THE WORLD IS TOO BIG, AND GOD'S
LOVE IS TOO GREAT TO LIVE JUST AN ORDINARY LIFE!

Friday, September 19, 2025

GOD, I HAVE TO THANK YOU

Dear God, I have to thank You today,
For looking beyond my faults, come what may.
For loving me with an unconditional heart,
And forgive me when I fail to do my part.

Forgive me when I don't love the same,
When I let my judgments cloud Your name.
Give me eyes to see beyond the strife,
To see the needs of others' difficult lives.

Help me to love as You have shown,
To meet their needs, to make You known.
Show me the way that pleases You,
In every act today, and in all I do.

Grant me patience, grant me grace,
To see Your light in every face.
For in Your love, I find my way,
To love others, day by day.

Thank You, God, for Your endless care,
For the love You give, it's always there.
Help me to mirror Your love so true,
In everything today that I say and do.

THE POOREST PERSON ON EARTH WHO IS FRIENDS WITH
GOD IS RICHER THAN THE RICHEST PERSON WHO IS NOT
FRIENDS WITH GOD!

Saturday, September 20, 2025

FAITH IS THE GREATEST FORCE

Faith is the greatest force on this earth,
Greater than hurricanes, bombs, or mirth.
What seems impossible in our sight,
Becomes possible with faith's pure light.

If we say, "It can't be done,"
We block the path before it's begun.
But if we declare, "It must be done,"
Then mountains move, and victories are won.

When we pray the Our Father, we proclaim,
"Thy will be done," in His holy name.
We don't say, "Thy will might be done,"
Or "Thy will can't be done," under the sun.

For faith transforms the impossible task,
It opens doors and removes the mask.
It empowers hearts to strive and achieve,
With faith, we trust, with faith, we believe.

"Thy will be done," we fervently pray,
Guiding our steps, lighting our way.
With faith, we conquer, with faith, we see,
The boundless possibilities of what can be.

PRAY, THEN LET IT GO. DON'T TRY TO MANIPULATE OR
FORCE THE OUTCOME. TRUST GOD TO OPEN THE RIGHT
DOORS AT THE RIGHT TIME!

Sunday, September 21, 2025

THE MASTER CRAFTSMAN

Whether we know it or not, Jesus is the key,
In our lives, He's the one we've sought desperately.
When something breaks and our spirits are torn,
We turn to Jesus, and we are reborn.

He is the Master Craftsman of all time,
Fixing the broken with love so sublime.
He takes the pieces and makes them anew,
With Jesus, we're better, whole again, and true.

In moments of darkness, when hope seems lost,
We lean on His grace, no matter the cost.
He guides us gently, through each troubled day,
With Jesus beside us, we'll find our way.

In His embrace, we find comfort and peace,
With Jesus, our burdens and sorrows cease.
Through every trial, He's there by our side,
With Jesus, we no longer need to hide.

So let us give thanks for His endless grace,
For the joy and love that fill our space.
With Jesus, our Savior, we stand tall and strong,
For in His love, we forever belong.

TO FALL IN LOVE WITH JESUS IS THE GREATEST
ROMANCE IN THE WORLD!

Monday, September 22, 2025

IN GOD'S EYES, WE'RE EQUALLY PRIZED

God never intended His boundaries to be small,
But to encompass the world, to include us all.
Yet you and I, we seek a gated ground,
Building walls and fences all around.

We try to keep safe from the rest of His kin,
Separate from those who are not within.
But when a hurricane hits, fierce and grand,
Both rich and poor feel it's devastating hand.

The gated communities and fences fall,
Reminding us we're one, after all.
For none of us hold a monopoly on God's love,
It's a gift, free from above.

In God's eyes, we're equally prized,
No walls, no gates, just open skies.
For God's love knows no boundary or fence,
It's boundless, pure, and immense.

So let us break down the walls we've built,
Embrace each other, and be free from guilt.
For in unity, we find His grace,
A world of love, in His embrace.

SOMETHING IS SERIOUSLY WRONG WHEN THE WORLD IS
OFFENDED BY EVERYTHING BUT LIARS AND SINNERS!

THE VOICE OF GOD

The voice of God opens your horizons wide,
While the enemy pins you, with nowhere to hide.
Where the good spirit gives hope to your soul,
The bad spirit sows doubts, anxiety takes its toll.

The good spirit calls you to love and serve,
To walk the right path, with courage and verve.
It appeals to your heart, to do good, to give,
Strengthening your resolve, inspiring you to live.

Conversely, the bad spirit encloses you tight,
Makes you rigid, intolerant, devoid of light.
It is the spirit of fear, of constant grievance,
Turning joy into sadness, faith into reluctance.

It makes you fearful, irritable, and bleak,
Enslaving your spirit, making your will weak.
The voice of God whispers, "Go forth, be brave,"
In the present, the future, there's much to save.

Choose the voice that brings light to your way,
That guides you gently through each day.
For the spirit of love, of hope, and of grace,
Will always open your heart to a brighter place.

WHATEVER IT IS, JUST TALK TO GOD ABOUT IT!

EMBRACE ALL THAT YOU ARE

You are not your age, nor your weight or hair,
Not just a name or dimples so fair.
You are all the words you choose to speak,
The smiles you share, the joy in laughter's peak.

You are every tear that's ever fallen,
All the places where your heart's been called in.
You're the things you believe with fervent might,
And the people you love and hold ever so tight.

You're the dreams of a future bright and clear,
The hopes you hold, the things you hold dear.
Remember always what you're not defined by,
But by the essence that makes your spirit fly.

You are not the labels the world may give,
But the love you spread, the life you live.
You are the courage in every step you take,
The strength in the choices you make.

So embrace all that you are, every part,
For you are a masterpiece, a work of the heart.
Don't forget the beauty that lies within,
The wondrous person you've always been.

GOD LOVES YOU MORE IN A SECOND THAN ANYONE
COULD IN A LIFETIME!

THE POWER OF SOMETHING SMALL

Sometimes it takes just a little bit of love,
To redeem a situation, a gift from above.
A little bit of grace, to heal a heart in need,
Just a tiny gesture, a simple, kind deed.

Sometimes it takes just a little bit of care,
To bring about a change, a kindness to share.
A little bit of patience, to work with those we meet,
Small acts of compassion, make our lives complete.

Never underestimate the power of something small,
The size of a mustard seed, can grow mighty and tall.
In the little things we do, great miracles can start,
For a little bit of love can change the human heart.

A smile can brighten a day that's dark and gray,
A word of encouragement can show the way.
A hand outstretched in friendship, a listening ear,
These small acts of kindness, can wipe away a tear.

So let us sow the seeds, with love and with grace,
With patience and kindness, in every time and place.
For it's the little things that often make the way,
To brighter tomorrows, from the deeds we do today.

SOMETIMES GOD DOESN'T CHANGE YOUR SITUATION
BECAUSE GOD IS TRYING TO CHANGE YOUR HEART!

Friday, September 26, 2025

THE MOST DIFFICULT WORD TO SAY IN LIFE

What is the most difficult word to say in life?
Not words of anger, nor words of strife.
I'd say the hardest word we try to defy,
The one that hurts the most, is the word "Good-bye."

We avoid saying "Good-bye" whenever we can,
For finality is hard for every woman and man.
There's something in us that yearns for more,
Hoping relationships and moments endure.

Centuries ago, words held deep meaning,
"God be with you" was the phrase worth gleaning.
In time contracted, simpler and dry,
The heartfelt blessing turned into "Good-bye."

So when you say "Good-bye," remember its start,
A blessing of love, from deep in the heart.
For though it may signal an end or a pause,
"Good-bye" holds within it, a divine cause.

So embrace "Good-bye" with a heart full of grace,
For it's not just an end, but a new start to face.
With "God be with you" hidden within,
"Good-bye" is where new journeys begin.

WITH GOD, LOVE STORIES NEVER END. THEY ARE MADE
ALIVE BECAUSE OF GOD'S POWER WITHIN US!

Saturday, September 27, 2025

THE TAPESTRY OF LIFE

We need to know who we are, and who others are too,
What makes us tick, and what others go through.
Grasping our hearts, and the hearts of our peers,
We find common ground, and alleviate our fears.

Knowing where we come from, and where others begin,
Helps us relate better, and let's kindness in.
With compassion, we bridge every divide,
Seeing the world from the other side.

For in understanding, our bonds grow strong,
With more kindness and patience, we all get along.
So let's learn about others, and ourselves every day,
In a world full of love, let empathy lead the way.

When we open our hearts to another's plight,
We bring hope and comfort, we spread the light.
Each story we hear, each struggle we find,
Adds depth to our spirit, enriches our mind.

So let us commit to this noble quest,
To know and to care, to give our best.
For in knowing each other, we find our true part,
In the tapestry of life, sewn heart to heart.

BEFORE GOD, WE ARE ALL EQUALLY WISE…..AND
EQUALLY FOOLISH!

Sunday, September 28, 2025

JESUS BORE THE SIN OF ADAM

Adam, after his sin, felt deep shame,
Naked and burdened, sensing the blame.
The weight of his actions, so heavy to bear,
Yet God did not leave him in total despair.

"Adam, where are you?" God sought him out,
In his moment of guilt, in his moment of doubt.
God's love was present, even in the Fall,
A reminder of grace, which is extended to all.

Jesus took on our nakedness, our shame,
He bore the sin of Adam, and all who came.
He washed away the guilt, he cleansed every stain,
Through His sacrifice, we are made whole again.

By the wounds of Jesus, healing has come,
A victory over sin, in God's earthly kingdom.
In His love and mercy, we find our place,
Redeemed and restored, by His infinite grace.

Through Jesus' sacrifice, we learn to forgive,
With His boundless love, we can now truly live.
With hearts renewed, in His name we stand,
Guided by His gentle, ever loving hand.

JESUS IS NOT A PSYCHOLOGIST. HE IS A CARDIOLOGIST.
JESUS DOES NOT LISTEN TO WORDS. JESUS LISTENS TO
HEARTS.

Monday, September 29, 2025

GOD USES EACH MOMENT

There are no accidents in a Christian's life,
Just incidents in God's plan, beyond our strife.
Where you are today is no mere chance,
But part of God's design, a sacred dance.

God uses each moment, each situation we're in,
To shape and prepare us, to cleanse us from sin.
For the place He will lead us, into tomorrow's light,
Trust in His wisdom, even in the darkest night.

Though we may not understand the road ahead,
In God's loving plan, we are gently led.
With faith and patience, in His hands we rest,
For His plan for us is always the very best.

So embrace each trial, and every joyous day,
Knowing God is with you, guiding your way.
In His perfect timing, His purpose will unfold,
Trust in His promise, let His love be your hold.

When doubts arise and fears take flight,
Remember God's love, His power and might.
He's molding your future, with care so divine,
In His grand tapestry, your life will forever shine.

YOU KNOW IT IS TRUE LOVE WHEN THAT PERSON
BRINGS YOU CLOSER TO GOD!

Tuesday, September 30, 2025

A WORLD THAT'S FORGOTTEN TO WEEP

We live in a world that's forgotten to weep,
To feel compassion, in our hearts so deep.
A globalization of indifference spreads,
Depriving us of tears, where empathy treads.

Let us ask the Lord for the grace to cry,
Over our indifference, and the reasons why.
To weep for the cruelty toward women dear,
For migrants and the poor, ever living in fear.

In the silence of night, let our hearts be moved,
By the pain of others, may we be so proved.
With tears that fall, may we cleanse our sight,
To see their struggles, and join in their fight.

May our tears turn to rivers, washing away,
The hardness of hearts, the apathy's sway.
For in our weeping, compassion will bloom,
Bringing light and love, dispelling the gloom.

Oh Lord, grant us tears for a world in need,
To suffer with others, to plant empathy's seed.
Let our hearts be soft, let our spirits be kind,
In a world renewed, may true peace be what we find.

IF YOU LOOK AT THE WORLD, YOU WILL BE DISTRESSED.
IF YOU LOOK WITHIN, YOU WILL BE DEPRESSED. IF YOU
LOOK AT GOD, YOU WILL BE AT REST

Wednesday, October 1, 2025

EMBRACE THE NOW

Our peace of mind is found in the now,
Living in the present, and taking a bow.
Despite what happened yesterday or last year,
Or what may come tomorrow, far or near.

The present moment is where we reside,
Yet past problems and future concerns collide.
Dominating our thoughts, causing distress,
Anxious, frustrated, and feeling less.

Life is not a rehearsal for what's to come,
Now is the time, where we must hum.
This is the only moment where we have control,
To live fully, and we are able to console.

When our attention stays in the present,
We push out fear, our minds are pleasant.
To combat fear, the best strategy,
Is bringing your focus back to reality.

Embrace the now, let go of the past,
Future concerns, let them fly fast.
For peace of mind, live in today,
In the present moment, find your way.

ONCE YOU HIT A CERTAIN AGE, ALL YOU REALLY WANT
IS GOD, FAMILY, STABILITY AND PEACE!

Thursday, October 2, 2025

ANGELS FROM ABOVE

Our guardian angel, with wings so bright,
Shields us with love both day and night.
A heavenly guide, forever near,
Sent from above to calm our fear.

Gabriel came with a message of grace,
Asking Mary to take her place.
To bear the Savior, born to redeem,
Fulfilling God's most holy dream.

Michael stands firm, a warrior bold,
Helping us when evil takes hold.
With the sword of truth, he fights each day,
To keep all darkness far away.

Raphael, the angel of healing and care,
Mends the soul with a quiet prayer.
With hands of mercy, he restores our way,
Bringing health to both night and day.

Angels from above, in heaven's glow,
Guide and protect us wherever we go.
In every task, through joy or strife,
They lead us toward eternal life.

MY FRIEND, GOD IS STILL IN THE MIRACLE BUSINESS.
DON'T GIVE UP YET!

Friday, October 3, 2025

A PRAYER FOR PEACE

I am longing for peace within me and all around,
For peace in families, where love is found.
Peace in neighborhoods, and between every nation,
For mother earth, and her sacred creation.

Peace in the quiet depths of my soul,
A serenity that makes me feel whole.
Peace for friends who face depression's strife,
And loved ones living through divorce and life.

Peace for those who lack the means they need,
For those who struggle, hearts that bleed.
Peace for the ones whose fears came true,
Who weep and sigh, their pain in full view.

I pray that a Spirit of peace and hope,
Will blow a breath of balm, and help us cope.
Upon every wound, may relief be near,
Bringing comfort, dispelling fear.

May there be a peace that surpasses all,
A divine calm that ever stands tall.
In every heart and in every land,
May peace spread with a gentle hand.

OUR COUNTRY DESPERATELY NEEDS CPR – CHRIST,
PRAYER AND REPENTENCE!

Saturday, October 4, 2025

THE PRAYER OF ST. FRANCIS

Lord, make me an instrument of Your peace,
Where hatred dwells, let love increase.
Where there's offense, let pardon reign,
And heal with grace where there's been pain.

Where doubt is strong, plant seeds of faith,
And in despair, bring hope to stay.
Where darkness grips, send forth Your light,
To banish shadows from the night.

Where sorrow lingers, joy impart,
To lift the burdened, broken heart.
O Master, help me seek to console,
To comfort others and make them whole.

Let me not seek to be understood,
But to understand, and seek the good.
Help me to love, not seek return,
For love is pure when freely earned.

In giving, we receive in grace,
In pardoning, we find our place.
And when we die, we're born anew,
To endless life with joy in You.

LEAVE ROOM FOR GOD TO SEND YOU ON DETOURS,
BECAUSE THE BLESSINGS MAY COME ON THE PATHS
THAT YOU DIDN'T EXPECT!

Sunday, October 5, 2025

JESUS, OUR PERFECT PRIZE

We often compare ourselves to other people
Believing we're better, and they are feeble.
We see others as less, to comfort our mind,
Keeping our self-image intact, or so we find.

"At least I'm not like so-and-so," we say,
But this comparison leads us astray.
For measuring worth by those we see,
Uses the wrong stick, incorrectly.

We gauge ourselves by imperfect souls,
A prototype flawed, it's full of holes.
Instead, our measure should be divine,
By comparing us to Jesus, pure and fine.

Only Jesus shows us the one true way,
In His example, we should ever stay.
For His life, perfect and just,
Is the measure in which to trust.

Let's turn our eyes to His light,
And in His reflection, find what's right.
No longer compare to human guise,
But look to Jesus, our perfect prize

JESUS ENTERS YOUR LIFE, SCANS YOUR PROBLEMS,
EDITS YOUR TENSIONS, DOWNLOADS YOUR SOLUTIONS,
DELETES YOUR WORRIES AND SAVES YOU!

THE GHOST OF REGRET

Regret is one of the ghosts of aging,
It prods us back, our past engaging.
Presses us to question every deed,
Every path taken, and our life's every seed.

"I should have stayed in school," we say,
"I should have exercised more each day.
I should have waited to marry my love,
Or majored in something else, but push came to shove."

"I should have changed jobs, sought something new,
Spent more time with family, bid old habits adieu.
I should have left this place, sought out fresh air,"
Regret whispers loudly, but leads to despair.

Regret is exhausting, an endless race,
It denies the good, puts sorrow in place.
It fails to see the joys and the gains,
The love, the laughter, the sunshine and rains.

So let go of regret, embrace the now,
The choices we've made, we'll make it somehow.
For each step has led us to who we are,
The journey of our life, a bright shining star.

GOD HAS PERFECT TIMING, NEVER EARLY, NEVER LATE!

LIFE'S TRUE VALUE

We realize that our lives are not our own,
In fleeting pleasures, we have often grown.
We overeat and then spend big bucks to trim,
While a billion starve, their chances are slim.

We live materialistic lives, filled with pride,
Thinking homes and stocks will forever rise.
Our possessions and money, we hold so tight,
Believing they are our lifelines, our guiding light.

But all lifelines have two ends, it's true,
We grasp and pull, but what does it do?
How secure is the other end, can we know?
In our grasping, do we let our true values show?

We must ponder the meaning of what we hold dear,
Is it wealth and goods, or love that's clear?
For in the end, when all is said and done,
It's the heart's true riches that outshine the sun.

So let's measure our worth by the love we give,
Not by the wealth we accumulate and live.
For life's true value is in the kindness we show,
In lifting others up, our true legacy will grow.

I AM NOT IN CONTROL, BUT I AM DEEPLY LOVED BY THE
ONE WHO IS!

FROM DOING TO BEING

The world's been upside down for so long,
It's hard to believe where we belong.
The meaning of life is not just in doing,
But in being, caring, and pursuing.

Being caring, being available, being true,
Being honest in all that we do.
Being interested, being spiritual,
Involved in life's moments, both big and small.

Many feel like pawns on a board,
Or cogs in a wheel, endlessly ignored.
To find meaning in the world around,
We must go deeper, where true joys are found.

More than just busy, more than just fast,
We must embrace moments that truly last.
From doing to being, we make our way,
Living fully in each and every precious day.

So let us pass from doing to being,
In every moment, truly seeing.
For in being, we find our true place,
A life of meaning, filled with grace.

TO SAY THAT I AM MADE IN THE IMAGE OF GOD IS TO
SAY THAT LOVE IS THE REASON FOR MY EXISTENCE, FOR
GOD IS LOVE!

A YEAR FROM NOW

Imagine what you're dealing with isn't here,
But a year from now, distant, not near.
Ask yourself, "Is it as important as it seems?"
Most of the time, it's less than it dreams.

An argument, mistake, lost keys in a rush,
A missed chance, a bruise from a sudden push.
A year from now, you won't even care,
Perspective will show it was light as air.

This thought brings the perspective you need,
To laugh at the things that make your heart bleed.
To see how minor these worries can be,
In the grand scheme of life, so wild and free.

So next time you're troubled, take a step back,
Picture a year from now, and cut yourself some slack.
You'll find yourself smiling at worries so slight,
Embracing the joy, letting go of the fight.

For life is too short to carry such weight,
Let go of the burdens, before it's too late.
In laughter and love, find peace in the now,
And look to the future with a lighter brow.

WHEN PEOPLE BRING UP YOUR PAST, TELL THEM: "JESUS
DROPPED THE CHARGES!"

Friday, October 10, 2025

THE ART OF LISTENING

Don't interrupt others, let them speak,
It takes much energy, in two heads to peek.
When you cut in, both thoughts intertwine,
Leaving nerves frayed, crossing a line.

You keep track of yours, and theirs as well,
A recipe for tension, as stories swell.
Both become nervous, annoyed and irate,
Patience in listening, we often underestimate.

We all resent when we're not truly heard,
When someone's attention wavers or is blurred.
Remind yourself to be patient, just wait,
Let them finish, their thoughts to create.

People will feel more relaxed in your space,
When you give them time, and grant them grace.
A good way to be more loving and kind,
Is to listen fully, with an open mind.

So practice the art of listening deep,
In conversations, let patience seep.
For in hearing others, we find our way,
To a more relaxed, and loving day.

LOVE IS GOD'S LANGUAGE WHICH REQUIRES NO SPOKEN
WORDS!

THE LIFE OF A PERFECTIONIST

The life of a perfectionist lacks inner peace,
For the quest for flawlessness never seems to cease.
The need for perfection and peace collide,
In this constant struggle, contentment is denied.

When things must be a certain way,
Better than they are, we stray.
Instead of gratitude for what we possess,
We fixate on flaws, and our minds obsess.

Zeroing in on what's wrong each day,
Dissatisfaction follows, leading us astray.
Focusing on imperfections, ours or others' we see,
We lose our ability to be gentle and free.

Attached to what's wrong, we miss what's right,
Insisting on change, we lose the light.
When you let go of the need for perfection,
You'll find peace in life's every section.

Embrace the present, let go of the quest,
For a life of peace is a life that's blessed.
Find joy in the moment, love in the now,
And inner peace will follow, this I vow.

THOSE WHO LEAVE EVERYTHING IN GOD'S HANDS WILL
EVENTUALLY SEE GOD'S HAND IN EVERYTHING!

CHAOS FOLLOWED JESUS

Chaos followed Jesus, drawn to His light,
The needy and sick sought His healing sight.
Those yearning for God, truth in their quest,
Flocked to Him, seeking peace and rest.

Like metal to a magnet, they were pulled near,
Creating a mob, bringing chaos and fear.
No one could shield Him from the pressing crowd,
Each soul seeking solace, many crying aloud.

The poor and downtrodden, His help they sought,
The sick and suffering, his healing they bought.
The lonely craved fellowship in His embrace,
Chaos ensued as He moved from place to place.

He stood up to power, both political and religious,
People marveled at His courage, so prestigious.
In Him, they saw truth, a beacon of grace,
Attracted to His spirit, they found their place.

In chaos and crowds, His love did shine,
Drawing people near, with a power divine.
Jesus, the light in a world so grim,
People were fascinated, and drawn to Him.

LORD, I NEED YOU MORE THAN EVER. PLEASE BRING
PEACE TO MY CONFUSION, JOY TO MY SADNESS AND
HOPE TO MY HEART!

Monday, October 13, 2025

THE HEART OF COMPASSION

Compassion is the art of stepping in another's shoes,
To take the focus off yourself, to feel and not to lose.
Imagine what it's like to be in someone else's plight,
To truly care and love them, to bring their pain to light.

It's realizing others' struggles are as real as your own,
Sometimes even worse, in ways we've never known.
By seeing their problems, their pain, their strife,
We open our hearts, and it enriches our life.

Compassion is doing small things with great love,
A gentle act of kindness, a message from above.
Jesus reaches out to those who suffer, in despair,
He walks beside them, even carries them with care.

When we offer help, we open up our hearts,
Enhancing gratitude, where true love starts.
In every act of kindness, big or small,
We mirror Jesus' love, embracing all.

So let us practice compassion, each and every day,
To touch a life with love, in a meaningful way.
For in the heart of compassion, we find our truest call,
To love as Jesus did, with open arms for all.

LOVE LIKE JESUS. CARE LIKE JESUS. BE SELFLESS LIKE
JESUS. FORGIVE LIKE JESUS. ENCOURAGE LIKE JESUS.
SERVE LIKE JESUS. BE PATIENT LIKE JESUS!

LIFE ISN'T FAIR

Life isn't fair, and that's liberating to know,
It's a truth we resist, but it's how life does go.
We make the mistake of thinking it should be,
That one day it will be fair for you and for me.

It's not and it won't be, that's just the way,
So we waste our time with complaints every day.
We commiserate with others, talk of life's wrongs,
Discussing the injustices, singing sad songs.

When we admit life's unfair, and stop feeling blue,
It frees us to do our best in all that we do.
Our job isn't to make everything right,
But to shine in the darkness, to bring forth the light.

When we see life's not fair, we gain a new view,
Compassion for others and ourselves, too.
Jesus taught this truth in His parable clear,
All workers were paid the same, no matter the sneer.

So let's embrace life, with all its flaws,
Doing our best, without even a pause.
For in this acceptance, we find peace and care,
A life full of love, aware that life's not fair.

GOD REACHES INTO THE DEEPEST PLACES IN YOUR
HEART AND GIVES YOU HIS PEACE!

THE EYES OF A STRANGER

We avoid eye contact with those we don't know,
Are we afraid, or just unsure of where to go?
It keeps our hearts closed, our smiles locked away,
From people we pass by every day?

Think of strangers as being a little like you,
With families, troubles, and fears they go through.
Treat them with kindness, respect, and a smile,
Do make eye contact, and linger a while.

You'll notice these strangers are a lot like you,
With concerns and joys, and dreams to pursue.
When you see the similarities, the innocence inside,
Inner happiness and joy won't be denied.

The Good Samaritan, with a heart so grand,
Helped a stranger, by lending a hand.
He felt joy and happiness, a peace so rare,
For in helping another, he found a love to share.

So open your heart to those you pass by,
With a smile and a glance, let kindness fly.
For in seeing others, as yourself you see,
A world filled with love, where hearts are free.

SOME DAYS, I ONLY HAVE TO STAND RIGHT WHERE I AM,
TO FEEL BLESSED BY GOD!

Thursday, October 16, 2025

MORALITY AND HUMAN VALUES

There is a lack of morality and human values today,
In society's rush for profit, we've lost our way.
Public life is seen as a struggle for power,
Morality cast aside, in a shadowy bower.

We need a new sense of brotherhood and care,
And a sisterhood that's just and fair.
Not self-righteous, nor exploitative in kind,
But a unity of heart, with peace in mind.

To bring more peace and wholeness we must strive,
To cast out greed, and let true values thrive.
Exploitation and indifference must be overcome,
With compassion and love, a new era begun.

For in our hands, we hold the power to heal,
To make a difference, to feel what others feel.
Let's foster a world where kindness leads,
And humanity flourishes through noble deeds.

With every step we take, with every hand we lend,
We shape a brighter future, a message we send.
That love and understanding are the paths to peace,
In a world united, where hostilities must cease.

LIFE IS FRAGILE. HANDLE WITH PRAYER!

Friday, October 17, 2025

LIFTING OTHERS UP

The reason we're tempted to put others down,
Is our ego believes it makes us strong, not a clown.
Correcting others to show they're wrong,
We think we'll feel better, and hopefully strong.

If you pay attention to how you feel,
After you've made someone else a big deal,
You'll notice a sadness, a weight in your heart,
For tearing others down is not a kind art.

Your compassionate heart knows what's true,
Hurting others won't bring any joy to you.
When you lift others up, and make them feel bright,
You share in their joy, and your heart feels light.

Jesus didn't need to agree to be kind,
With love and compassion, His heart was aligned.
So resist the urge to prove you're right,
And spread love and kindness, day and night.

For true contentment and peace of mind,
Comes from being gentle, thoughtful, and kind.
Instead of correction, offer a cheer,
And lift others up, spreading joy far and near.

SOMETIMES YOUR BLESSINGS COME TO YOU IN
MYSTERIOUS WAYS – THROUGH PAIN AND TROUBLE!

Saturday, October 18, 2025

JESUS IS GOD'S SMILE

When we look at a baby, we can't help but smile,
And if their small smile blooms, even for a while,
A deep, heartfelt emotion stirs inside,
A powerful connection we cannot hide.

While the child may respond to our loving gaze,
Their smile holds power, in so many ways.
Pure as spring water, it reflects innocence bright,
Awakening in us, a sheer nostalgic delight.

It brings back memories of our own carefree days,
Of laughter and joy in childhood's gentle ways.
This is what happened with Jesus and His kin,
A smile from Him brought love deep within.

A smile bloomed on the lips of the newborn divine,
Jesus, God's gift, it was a holy sign.
Jesus is God's smile, pure and true,
A message of love brought to me and you.

So when we see a baby's smile so sweet,
Let us remember the joy complete,
Of God's love sent from above,
In the smile of Jesus, ever a gift of love.

IF YOU FEEL INADEQUATE, WORTHLESS OR NOT
ENOUGH, YOU DIDN'T GET THOSE IDEAS FROM JESUS!

"WAIT" IS A CRUEL WORD

"Wait" is a cruel word for our frenzied world,
We're impatient, and our emotions whirled.
Why write it, when you can text it instead?
We expect instant results, instant action ahead.

Instant foods, we've got them in our hands,
So why not instant results, as life demands?
We can't wait; we want it all right now,
Patience is hard, but we must learn how.

Waiting for the Lord's guidance, His timing so hard,
But running ahead leaves us tired and scarred.
Without waiting on God, we have no power,
In haste, we destroy the beauty of each hour.

Like rushing the hatching of a bird or a chick,
Too soon, we destroy what should come quick.
When we run ahead of God's perfect design,
We miss out on the wonders that are sublime.

So let's slow down and learn to wait,
Trust in God's timing, it's never late.
In patience, we'll find strength and grace,
And see His perfect plan as it takes place.

AS A WELL-SPENT DAY BRINGS HAPPY SLEEP, SO A
WELL-LIVED LIFE BRINGS A HAPPY DEATH INTO THE
ARMS OF JESUS!

Monday, October 20, 2025

WHEN BATTLES CEASE

Life is rarely the way we want it to be,
Other people don't act as we'd like to see.
Moment to moment, some things bring delight,
While others frustrate us, and don't seem right.

There will always be those who disagree,
Who see things differently, just let them be.
Not everything will work out as planned,
Accept what comes, and understand.

If you fight against it all, you'll be worn thin,
Battles unending, so where to begin?
Decide which fights are worth your might,
And which to leave, fading from sight.

Most battles steal your inner peace,
Fighting small things that matter least.
People argue over trivial ties,
Missing the beauty before their eyes.

A day may come when battles cease,
A time of calm, a time of peace.
Jesus calmed the storm with, "Peace, be still,"
Find that peace within, and you'll have your fill.

YOU ARE JUST ONE HEARTBEAT AWAY FROM ETERNITY!

FINDING HOLINESS

Everything God created is potentially holy,
Our task is to find it, slowly and wholly.
It's easy to see in a sunrise so bright,
In snow-capped mountains or a child's delight.

But can we see God in a struggle or strife,
In moments of death, or the hardships of life?
When we seek God's holiness in everyday things,
A magical transformation begins and springs.

Remember this truth on a difficult day,
When dealing with people or bills we can't pay.
The beauty of God may be hidden from view,
But it's there, waiting, in everything we do.

The fact we can't see it doesn't mean it's not there,
We just need to look more closely, with care.
For holiness hides in the mundane and plain,
In joy and in sorrow, in pleasure and pain.

So open your heart and sharpen your sight,
To see the divine in the darkest of night.
In every situation, find the sacred and pure,
God's presence is constant, steadfast, and sure.

GOD CARES ABOUT THOSE IN NEED, AND SO SHOULD WE
IN GOD'S FAMILY!

NO ONE IS PERFECT

You can love someone but not always like them,
Go easy on yourself, you're only human.
And so is the other, no one is perfect,
Together you'll find, no reason to defect.

Everyone has good days and not-so-good days,
But working together, you'll find better ways.
Facing life's challenges, hand in hand,
You'll get through anything, do understand.

And remember, God is always near,
To help you along, to calm your fear.
In times of struggle, when skies are gray,
Hold on to each other, come what may.

For love isn't just joy, it's also the fight,
Together you'll shine, through the darkest night.
With faith and support, you'll find your way,
Together forever, come what may.

When doubt creeps in and shadows loom,
Your love will light up the darkest room.
With patience and care, you both will grow,
In each other's hearts, the love will show.

MAKE TIME FOR GOD AND SEE WHAT HAPPENS!

Thursday, October 23, 2025

GOD'S TAPESTRY FROM ON HIGH

Viewed from the one side, it's a work of art,
Threads of colors, each playing its part.
An inspiring picture, intricately designed,
But flip it over, and a mess you'll find.

A hodgepodge of threads, some short, some long,
Some smooth, some knotted, seeming all wrong.
Yet in this chaos, a pattern does fit,
God's intricate design, every bit of it.

Good people suffer, it's part of the plan,
Twisted, knotted lives, as only God can.
Not because one thread deserves more,
But each has a role, a life to explore.

From our view below, it seems a mess,
Rewards and punishments, causing distress.
But from above, in God's great view,
Every twist and knot has a purpose too.

God's tapestry, from His vantage on high,
Shows every life's thread, and the reason why.
In His grand design, each part plays a role,
A beautiful work, complete and whole.

THE WORK GOD DOES WITHIN YOU WHILE YOU WAIT IS
JUST AS IMPORTANT AS WHATEVER YOU'RE WAITING
FOR!

Friday, October 24, 2025

TRUE VIRTUE

Anxiety whispers, "You can't afford to share,"
"Your needs are many, your cupboards are bare."
In a world of fear, where shadows loom,
Vices we once scorned, become virtues in bloom.

Hoarding and greed, suspicion and strife,
Prudent they seem, in this anxious life.
Fear, not love, takes the lead,
In hearts where kindness used to breed.

True virtues turn from our sight,
Guiding us to love, in God's pure light.
But fear diverts us from this path,
Leading us to a safety that won't last.

For virtues that are born from fear,
Cannot bring us closer, and cannot endear.
They pull us from the true and good,
From loving God, as we should.

Let's cast aside these fears we hold,
And embrace the virtues, brave and bold.
Love of God and neighbor, true and kind,
In these, true peace we'll always find.

EVERY MORNING I SPEND FIFTEEN MINUTES FILLING MY
MIND FULL OF GOD, SO THERE'S NO ROOM LEFT FOR
WORRY THOUGHTS!

A GOD WHO SHAKES THE WORLD

During an earthquake, the village shook,
Everyone was wearing a fearful look.
But one old woman, calm and bright,
Showed joy and peace, in the night.

"Dear lady, aren't you afraid?" they cried,
With trembling voices, fear amplified.
"No," she answered, with a peaceful smile,
"I have a God who shakes the world with style."

Her faith so strong, unwavering, bold,
In God's great power, her trust did hold.
A God who can shake the earth and skies,
Yet brings peace, wherever fear lies.

Is your faith as strong, in storms untold?
Believing in a God who holds the world?
With trust in Him, find calm and peace,
In His great love, your fears release.

So in the face of trials, stand firm and true,
Let your faith be strong, let it renew.
For with a God who can shake the earth,
You'll find courage and know your worth.

I DID MY BEST AND GOD DID THE REST!

Sunday, October 26, 2025

WEAK PEOPLE GROW SO STRONG

I've seen weak people grow so strong,
Timid hearts find courage all along.
Selfish souls become so kind,
In acts of love, their strength we find.

Caring for elders, a brain-damaged kid,
For wives in wheelchairs, life isn't hid.
Years and decades, their love persists,
A strength from God, their hearts enlist.

Where do they find the will to endure?
A love so deep, in a heart so pure.
When weary and out of strength, we turn,
To God, for His power, our hearts do yearn.

God renews our spirit, He makes us strong,
So we can run and lift up our song.
We walk and don't faint, by His might,
In the darkest times, God is our light.

God puts us through what we can bear,
In the strongest struggles, He's always there.
Chosen to be strong, through the test,
In God's embrace, we find our rest.

AGING IS GOD'S IDEA. IT'S ONE OF THE WAYS GOD KEEPS
US HEADED HOME TO HIM!

SPEAK AND THEN LISTEN TO GOD

Talking to God is a two-way street,
Not just sending Him another tweet.
It's not just silence, waiting to see,
Prayer involves both you and He.

Speak your heart, then listen well,
As you go about your day, let your heart swell.
Like any friendship, talking's the key,
To grow closer to God, in His grace, you'll be.

We start by speaking, then listening still,
Watching for God's voice, seeking His will.
He may not answer as quickly as some,
But in due time, His answers will come.

Talk to God about what's on your mind,
The troubles and joys, the peace you find.
If your heart is right, seeking His way,
He'll guide and teach you, day by day.

So speak and listen, with a heart that's true,
God's always there, guiding you through.
In this two-way conversation, you'll see,
A closer walk with God, it's eternally free.

JESUS WAS GOD SPELLING HIMSELF OUT IN LANGUAGE
HUMANITY COULD UNDERSTAND!

RAISED TO BELIEVE

Raised to believe we're special, unique,
Meant to leave marks, profound and deep.
Yet we live in shadows, unseen and obscure,
Our significance seems far from secure.

We're taught our lives hold infinite worth,
Our dreams and loves, our pains and mirth.
But living in a world that can't relate,
We struggle to find our destined fate.

What happens when our stories dear,
Are met with boredom, that's not sincere?
When hearts that ache to share their tale,
Find only silence, and voices that are frail.

We feel the trap of unmet dreams,
A life that's less than what it seems.
Deprived of God, the source of peace,
Our restless hearts can find no ease.

Only in God, our true worth lies,
In prayer and love, our spirits rise.
Hidden in Christ, we find our place,
Our ache replaced by His tranquil grace.

GOD, YOU OWN THE SKIES AND THE STARS AND
STILL.....YOU WANT MY HEART!

THE DANCE OF SEASONS

Life has its seasons, a rhythmic dance,
Our hearts interwoven in nature's trance.
Spring brings warmth, autumn a sigh,
Winter's chill, and a summer's sky.

Moods that ebb, like the flow of the sea,
Complex yet simple, an eternal decree.
Living then dying, a cycle so grand,
A break in the rhythm, new life to expand.

A mystery, a wonder, so profound,
In life's joys, we become spellbound.
Day in and out, its joys we find,
Exultation in being, for body and mind.

Loving and sensing, each moment we seize,
Eating and being, life's simple pleas.
Underneath it all, a truth so clear,
The sheer joy of living, ever so near.

In the dance of seasons, we find our way,
Through night and dawn, through dusk and day.
With hearts that beat in nature's rhyme,
We cherish the gift of life, oh so sublime.

SPRING SHOWS US WHAT GOD CAN DO WITH A DRAB
WORLD!

SEE LIFE'S GIFTS AT EVERY TURN

One of the hardest things to do is celebrate,
We wish to, we need to, but we hesitate.
Celebration doesn't come with ease,
In our quest for joy, we miss the keys.

We overdo the things we daily partake,
Drinking, eating, and laughter we make.
Loving, talking, singing out loud,
All in excess, hoping joy is found.

We eat too much, drink in excess,
Sing so loudly, our happiness to express.
Yet joy eludes us in this frantic chase,
For true celebration, we often misplace.

The reason why we find it so tough,
Is we forget life's blessings are enough.
Pleasure, love, enjoyment as gifts bestowed,
From God above, from His heavenly abode.

To truly celebrate, we must learn,
To see life's gifts at every turn.
Taking joy in simple, pure delight,
In gratitude, our hearts do take flight.

IF GOD ALWAYS MET YOUR EXPECTATIONS, GOD WOULD
NEVER HAVE TO EXCEED THEM!

Friday, October 31, 2025

Halloween

REMOVE YOUR DISGUISE

Be brave enough to remove your disguise,
To see who you are beneath your eyes.
Embrace your flaws, they make you real,
They show the world how deeply you feel.

Be vulnerable and accept each part,
Every imperfection is a work of art.
These make you human, they make you whole,
They reflect the depth of your unique soul.

Be confident in your strengths each day,
Don't hide your gifts or shy away.
Share with the world your light so bright,
For your talents bring others pure delight.

Say with courage, "This is me,"
Embrace mistakes, let them set you free.
Forgetful and messy, yet doing your best,
In every struggle, you find your zest.

Proud of who you are and will be,
Becoming the person you're meant to see.
In every flaw and strength combined,
Lies a journey of beauty, one of a kind.

MOST OF GOD'S ANGELS COME TO US IN DISGUISE!

Saturday, November 1, 2025

All Saints Day

A SAINT LIVES A LIFE OF SERVICE

A saint lives not for self alone,
But for the love that Christ has shown.
Though flawed and human, they still pursue
A life in service, strong and true.

Set apart for God's design,
Their hearts align with love divine.
They aren't perfect, but through the strife,
God's glory shines within their life.

They stumble, sin, and fall from grace,
Yet rise again to seek God's face.
For in their weakness, strength is found,
As mercy lifts them from the ground.

They give their lives for Jesus' name,
To serve the lost, to bear the flame.
With every step, His call they have heard,
And follow closely to spread His word.

God's light pours through their every deed,
In sacrifice, they plant a seed.
Though not without mistakes or flaws,
They live for Christ and serve His cause.

GOD COMFORTS THE DISTURBED AND DISTURBS THE
COMFORTABLE!

Sunday, November 2, 2025

All Souls Day

THE LOSS OF SOMEONE DEAR

Imagine the loss of someone dear,
A heart in pain, filled with fear.
Hurt so deep, it's all you see,
You go to pray, seeking to be free.

Temptation pulls to focus within,
To talk it through, to maybe dwell on sin.
But this path leads to deeper despair,
Fixing on pain, your heart to snare.

Instead, turn your gaze to God above,
Focus on His mystery, His boundless love.
In Christ's life, let your heart find light,
Your depression will break, your soul take flight.

A wounded child in its mother's embrace,
Finds strength and comfort, grace upon grace.
Climb into God's lap, feel the shift,
Your heart will heal, with a gentle lift.

Let God's love overshadow your plight,
Bringing peace through the darkest night.
For in His presence, you will see,
Your pain becomes significantly free.

IN MANY WAYS, AGING WELL IS ABOUT LEARNING TO
LET GO OF EARTHLY THINGS AND CLING TO GOD ALONE!

Monday, November 3, 2025

OUR PRESENCE SPEAKS

Sometimes we help the most, it's true,
When there's nothing we can really do.
In moments when we're lost for words,
Our presence speaks, though nothing's heard.

At funerals, we stand in place,
With helpless hearts, in silent grace.
No words can heal a grieving soul,
But being there can make them whole.

It's strange, but in our helplessness,
We offer more by doing less.
When we can't fix, or say what's right,
Our quiet presence brings the light.

For in the space where we can't strive,
God's grace alone can come alive.
When efforts fail, His love flows through,
Uncolored by the things we do.

So when we feel we're lost, unsure,
Know that in stillness, we're so very pure.
It's in our helplessness we find,
God's grace at work, ever soft and kind.

I DON'T REALIZE THAT JESUS IS ALL I NEED, UNTIL JESUS
IS ALL I HAVE!

Tuesday, November 4, 2025

POLITICS DEMANDS INVOLVEMENT

For many, politics is a dirty word,
Of dishonesty and power absurd.
Misused and twisted, self-interest reigns,
Propaganda spreads and truth refrains.

The temptation to avoid it is strong,
To disengage, and to avoid the wrong.
But politics, despite all its sin,
Demands involvement, so we must dig in.

No Christian can afford to hide,
Community needs us to decide.
For without politics, we're left alone,
Victims of fate, we're on paths unknown.

Effective politics forms the heart,
Of every community's vital part.
It provides structures that protect and guide,
So that we can all live side by side.

Community depends on this,
A shaped future, not hit or miss.
To gather, celebrate, and educate,
Politics always steers our common fate.

GOD ANSWERS KNEE-MAIL!

Wednesday, November 5, 2025

COLD INDIFFERENCE

A lady leaves a restaurant, winter's chill in the air,
Wrapped in a fur coat, a vision of wealth and care.
At the door, a woman sits, shivering on a crate,
Poorly dressed, hand outstretched, facing a cruel fate.

Indifference bulletproofs the wealthy woman's soul,
Making it hard to look over, taking its toll.
Certain sights just bounce away,
Leaving her heart cold, leading her astray.

One of the dangers of this cold indifference,
Is how it seeps into life, always in silence.
Silently shaping our judgments and ways,
Turning warm hearts into a cold, indifferent haze.

We cannot get used to this, the silent freeze,
We must awaken, helping our hearts to seize.
To see the shivering, the outstretched hand,
To feel the call, is to understand.

Indifference must not become our norm,
We must keep our hearts tender, and warm.
To care, to share, to give, to hold,
Is the way to keep our souls from the cold.

MY LIFE IS FILLED WITH BROKEN PIECES, TERRIBLE
CHOICES AND UGLY TRUTHS. IT'S ALSO FILLED WITH A
MAJOR COMEBACK, PEACE IN MY SOUL, AND GRACE
THAT SAVED MY LIFE!

Thursday, November 6, 2025

TURN THE OTHER CHEEK

In the halls where power sways,
Where voices clash in loud array,
A figure stands amidst the strife,
A politician, versed in life.

With words that cut and promises deep,
He speaks to those who dare to weep,
Yet when the stones of scorn are thrown,
He turns his cheek, a stance well-known.

"Forgive," he says, with voice so clear,
"Let love replace the seed of fear."
His rivals mock, they plot, they scheme,
But he holds fast to a higher dream.

So in this realm where tempests roar,
Where greed and pride take hold and soar,
Remember this, in heart and mind,
True strength is gentle, just, and kind.

For the politician who seeks to lead,
Must plant a humble, righteous seed,
And in the storm, though fierce and bleak,
He'll stand tall, and turn the other cheek.

GOD DOESN'T DESIGN ACCIDENTS, GOD CREATES
PURPOSES!

WRESTLING WITH THE DIVINE

In wrestling with the divine we find,
A challenge for the heart and mind.
God welcomes questions, doubts, and fear,
Inviting us to ever draw Him near.

With sleeves rolled up, God meets our fight,
Encouraging us to seek the light.
Our struggles, cries, and pleas unfold,
A dance of trust, both fierce and bold.

We grapple with our faith and fate,
In moments when our hearts hesitate.
Yet in this match, we come to know,
The depths of love that God will show.

For those who wrestle and engage,
Find blessings that their fears assuage.
A new name given, a strength reborn,
Through trials faced and spirits worn.

This is the battle where we learn,
To trust in God and, in return,
Embrace the will that God imparts,

MANY FOLKS WANT TO SERVE GOD, BUT ONLY AS GOD'S
ADVISORS!

THE GIFT OF GIVING

A poor man on the snowy street did plead,
To a wealthy man for some small need.
"Loose change," he asked, his voice so low,
A simple gift, to get him an espresso.

The rich man paused, and from his hand,
A considerable sum, it was truly grand.
A friend inquired, puzzled by the sight,
"Why give so much? Coins would be alright."

"Coins," said the rich man, "meet his need,
But this gift answers a different creed.
To give without measure, without restraint,
Brings me such joy, without any constraint."

Jesus' words rang clear, so erudite,
"What you've received, give with all your might.
As a gift it came, now as a gift depart,
From hand to hand, from heart to heart."

The poor man, grateful, his eyes aglow,
Felt a warmth, despite all the snow.
The wealthy man, with his heart so light,
Found in giving, such pure delight.

INSTEAD OF COMPLAINING, ASK GOD: "WHAT IS THE
LESSON YOU'RE TRYING TO TEACH ME, DEAR GOD?"

Sunday, November 9, 2025

FROM THE DAY JESUS WAS BORN

From the day Jesus was born, his presence here,
He chased away demons that thrived on fear.
He didn't discuss what politicians say,
"Give to Caesar what's Caesar's" was his only way.

He spoke of forgiveness, seven times seventy,
Of turning the other cheek, and love's true identity.
Unlike the voices that shout and fight,
Jesus taught love as the path to the light.

Those who claim wisdom are far from his word,
And demons in freedom have taken the world.
They strive to divide, to conquer, to rule,
But ask yourself this: What would Jesus do?

He'd call for compassion, for peace to renew,
For hearts to be open, for love to be true.
In a world full of chaos, we must seek the clue,
What would Jesus say? And what would Jesus do?

With love as our guide, we find our way through,
And strive to be better in all that we do.
For though the world struggles with darkness in view,
We'll follow his teachings and his love we'll pursue.

REMEMBER IF YOU'RE HEADED IN THE WRONG
DIRECTION, GOD ALLOWS FOR U-TURNS!

THE WAITING ROOM

There is not a place with more waiting on earth,
Than the intensive care waiting room, where fear has birth.
Urgent questions fill the air, each breath a silent plea,
Will my husband make it? Will my child walk free?

In this waiting room, the world seems to pause,
Where kindness blooms without applause.
Distinctions of class and race melt away,
As hearts unite in hopes that sway.

A father's love, a garbage man's tears,
A professor's prayers, confronting their fears.
Each person pulls for the others there,
In that room, there's only love and hope to share.

The universe narrows to a single thought,
A doctor's report, the hope they've sought.
In this space, life's true meaning is clear,
To love and support those we hold so dear.

How we could learn to truly love each day,
If we lived like the waiting room was our way.
For every moment is a chance to care,
Another day in the waiting room, if we dare.

GOD CREATED HEAVEN AND EARTH IN ONE DAY. WHO'S
TO SAY GOD CANNOT CHANGE YOUR LIFE IN ONE DAY?

Tuesday, November 11, 2025

MOTHER TERESA AND THE LOVE FOR JUST ONE

Mother Teresa once said, "It's not about the masses,
But the love for just one that truly surpasses.
I can care for just one, one soul at a time,
To lift up a heart and help it to climb.

"If I hadn't picked up that one person there,
I wouldn't have reached 42,000 with care.
My work's just a drop in the ocean's wide sprawl,
Yet without that one drop, it wouldn't be full at all."

One by one, she showed us the way,
To love with our hearts and brighten the day.
The ocean's made full by each little part,
A single drop of love is where we should start.

So look to the person you can touch right now,
With a kind word or smile, or a gentle vow.
Begin with just one, as Mother Teresa knew,
For each small act of love adds something new.

It's not in the grand, but in the little things,
Where the Spirit soars and the heart truly sings.
In the ripple of kindness, where the ocean grows wide,
Each and every drop of compassion joins the tide.

ACT IN SUCH A MANNER THAT YOU ARE LIVING PROOF
OF A LOVING GOD!

Wednesday, November 12, 2025

HOPE GUIDES US ONWARD

Hope is not simple optimism, denying what's amiss,
Nor wishful thinking, dreaming of future bliss.
Hope isn't a blind belief that all will be alright,
Or a way to ignore the darkness of the night.

Hope doesn't depend on the news of the day,
Whether good or bad, it won't fade away.
For hope looks beyond the present news,
And sees a promise that forever renews.

Hope sees the facts, but it trusts in the plan,
A vision of life in the hands of the great I AM.
With eyes open wide, it faces the storm,
Knowing in God's promise, it will transform.

In a world where chaos can reign supreme,
Hope finds the truth in a greater dream.
It doesn't deny what the world may say,
But hope trusts in God's love, come what may.

Hope lives in the heart that chooses to see,
The promise of God, the ultimate decree.
So no matter what happens, no matter the night,
Hope guides us onward, always towards the light.

WE SAY, "SHOW ME AND I'LL TRUST YOU." GOD SAYS,
"TRUST ME AND I'LL SHOW YOU!"

Thursday, November 13, 2025

A BOX OF KISSES

In a moment of anger, the father scolded his girl,
For wasting the wrapping paper, all shiny and swirl.
Money was tight, and his patience ran thin,
Yet she offered a gift, with a sweet, loving grin.

With a father's frustration, he opened the box,
Finding it empty, his temper still talks.
"Don't you know gifts should hold something inside?"
His words made her teary, her joy had been denied.

With tears in her eyes, she looked up and said,
"It's full of my kisses, just for you, Dad."
His heart melted quickly, realizing his wrong,
Embracing his daughter, where love is lifelong.

That box, now a treasure, he kept it close by,
A reminder of the love, that money can't buy.
In moments of doubt, he'd reach for her kiss,
From the box with gold paper, a daughter's pure bliss.

Through years it stayed near, a symbol so true,
Of the power of love, in all we pursue.
For what seemed empty, was filled to the brim,
With the heart of a child, and love's precious hymn.

DEAR GOD, PLEASE HELP ME TO RESPOND WITH LOVE
BEFORE I REACT WITH ANGER!

Friday, November 14, 2025

OLD AGE CAN BE A GOLDEN TIME

Old age can be a golden time of delight,
Where wisdom's light shines ever so bright.
I cherish the years that have enriched my soul,
With sweet and bitter moments that make me whole.

My faith now confirmed, a treasure so grand,
Exceeding the youthful hopes I once had planned.
The love of God fills my heart with peace,
A gift that brings joy and a sweet release.

These are the best years of my life, they say,
The birds sing sweeter, the path is clear each day.
The winds whisper softly, the sun's radiant glow,
Illuminates my spirit, and makes my heart grow.

Though my outward form may slowly fade,
Inside, a vibrant renewal is constantly made.
I embrace the journey, every step of the way,
With gratitude for blessings that grace my day.

For in this season, the soul finds rest,
With lessons learned and moments blessed.
Old age, a time of fulfillment and grace,
A testament to life's enduring embrace.

LIFE IS WAY TOO SHORT TO SPEND ANOTHER DAY AT
WAR WITH YOURSELF! – GOD

Saturday, November 15, 2025

I KNOW YOU ARE ALL MINE

One Saturday morning, a mother sat,
In old slacks with her hair unkempt and flat.
Her young son smiled, his eyes so bright,
And said, "Mommy, you're so pretty today, a lovely sight!"

She chuckled and asked, "Are you teasing me?
I'm a sight with no makeup, can't you see?
Monday through Friday, I'm dressed to impress,
But today, my dear, I'm looking like such a mess."

The boy replied with innocence and cheer,
"When you look like that, you're always out of here,
But when you look like this, with no need to roam,
I know you are all mine, right here at home!"

We all seek someone to be ours alone,
To feel special and loved, down to the bone.
Just like that child, with a heart so pure,
Yearning for a love that's simple and sure.

It's not about beauty or fancy attire,
It's the warmth of presence that we desire.
To be loved by Someone who's truly divine,
And know, in those moments, they are all mine.

GOD CARES A LOT MORE ABOUT WHAT'S IN YOUR
HEART THAN WHAT'S IN YOUR FRIDGE!

Sunday, November 16, 2025

TO LOVE ONE ANOTHER

In studying Jesus' life, there is so much to do,
An eternity of lessons and guidance so true.
But in His teachings, one command shines bright:
To love one another with all of our might.

We are called to cherish and hold each other dear,
To lay down our lives without any fear.
For in this love, we find our true role,
An extension of the vine, which makes us whole.

Jesus knew that love would pave the way,
And through His command, we find our stay.
For if we can love, all else will align,
In the heart of the Savior, who is the true vine.

Through acts of kindness and words of grace,
We reflect the love of Jesus' embrace.
In loving others, we fulfill His plan,
To bring unity and peace to every man.

Let us hold on to His command, and forever be,
A beacon of love for all to see.
In loving one another, we truly shine,
Living as branches of Jesus, the true vine.

PEOPLE WATCH YOU SURVIVING AND WONDER WHY
YOU HAVEN'T LOST YOUR MIND. MAKE SURE YOU TELL
THEM…..JESUS!

AT YOUR DOOR

Often what we seek is close at hand,
Right under our noses, in our own land.
Blinded by lures of something new,
We miss the blessings in clear view.

The Prodigal Son sought fortune and fame,
In far-off lands, he played the game.
He lost his joy, his life content,
In search of riches, his heart was spent.

In distant lands, excitement he chased,
But found his life was truly misplaced.
He realized, in time, what he had missed,
His father's love, the true bliss.

Don't search for joy in distant places,
For blessings lie in familiar faces.
What you seek might be very near,
In your own home, where love is clear.

Look around, see what you possess,
In simple things, find happiness.
For what you need, and all you adore,
Is often right where you are, at your door.

LOVE AND COMPASSION ARE THE HIGHEST FORMS OF
INTELLIGENCE GIVEN TO US BY GOD!

TEACHING US TRUST

In Portugal stands a monastery high,
Perched on a cliff that touches the sky.
To reach its heights, a basket you ride,
Pulled by monks, with faith as your guide.

An American tourist, halfway in fright,
Saw the rope was old, not looking right.
He asked the monk, to calm his fear,
"How often replaced?" he needed to hear.

The monk replied, with a steady tone,
"We change it when it breaks," on its own.
Not the words of comfort the tourist sought,
But truth sometimes is not what we thought.

God's words to us can be much the same,
Not always comforting, nor always tame.
Yet in His wisdom, there's guidance true,
Teaching us trust, in all we pursue.

So in life's journey, with faith we steer,
Facing fears, even when it's unclear.
For God's messages, though hard to take,
Are given in love, for our own sake.

FAITH IS LIKE WI-FI, IT'S INVISIBLE, BUT IT HAS THE
POWER TO CONNECT YOU TO THE GOD YOU NEED!

Wednesday, November 19, 2025

COUNT YOUR BLESSINGS

Lord, thank you for this sink of dirty dishes,
For the bounty of food that fills our wishes.
Thank you for the pile of laundry so high,
For the clothes we wear with a satisfied sigh.

Thank you for the taxes I must pay,
And the job that employs me every day.
Thank you for the mess after a party,
And friends who make my life so hearty.

Thank you for clothes a bit too snug,
After lots of cookies and my coffee mug.
Thank you for complaints about our land,
A result of free speech and rights that stand.

Thank you for my muscles weary and sore,
For the work I accomplish and so much more.
Thank you for mornings so loud and wild,
For the love and laughter of my family and child.

Thank you for the table messy and bare,
For the meals we've shared with love and care.
Thank you for all the gifts you've given,
For a life so full and a heart that's risen.

COUNTING YOUR BLESSINGS IS BETTER THAN
RECOUNTING YOUR PROBLEMS!

Thursday, November 20, 2025

WE'RE TIRED AND WEARY

We are tired of politicians who fail to deliver,
And weary of entertainment that leaves us to shiver.
Exhausted by neighbors entangled in strife,
Disenchanted by religion that gives stones, not life.

We're worn out by conflicts with no resolution,
And weary of promises without execution.
Yet God instills hope deep within our hearts,
And a trust in a world where true healing starts.

Love, truth, and integrity will never be defeated,
For in our hearts, God's kingdom is seeded.
Though kingdoms of earth may falter and sway,
God's Kingdom will come, as we faithfully pray.

In each prayer we utter, in each hope we keep,
We trust in a promise that runs true and deep.
For the world is not as it seems at first glance,
God's love and truth give us a fighting chance.

So we stand with faith, with courage anew,
Embracing the vision that God makes true.
In a world transformed by love's divine art,
We find our peace, within each soul and heart.

GOD IS ALWAYS WITH YOU.....YOU JUST NEED TO PAY
ATTENTION!

TWO PLUS TWO FOREVER EQUALS FOUR

Our sanity depends on knowing what is true,
For when truth crumbles, chaos does ensue.
If two plus two should equal three,
The foundation of sanity will cease to be.

Our personal and social sanity rely,
On truths we acknowledge, the truths we imply.
In a world where truth is steadfast and sure,
Two plus two forever equals four.

The danger resides in hiding ourselves with lies,
Covering our weakness with a deceitful guise.
For Satan, the Prince of Lies, deceives,
And the web of falsehood he constantly weaves.

To live in truth is a moral call,
To stand with courage, never to fall.
For truth is the anchor that keeps us whole,
Binding together our body and soul.

Let us speak truth in all that we do,
To keep our hearts and our minds ever true.
In a world that shifts and constantly lies,
Let us hold fast to truth's guiding ties.

ALWAYS BELIEVE IN GOD, BECAUSE THERE ARE SOME
QUESTIONS THAT EVEN GOOGLE CAN'T ANSWER!

Saturday, November 22, 2025

TWO MEN MET AFTER FIFTY LONG YEARS

Two men who were once so close and dear,
Met again after fifty long years.
With grins and a handshake, they hugged with delight,
Rekindling a friendship that once felt so right.

They reminisced about days filled with cheer,
Laughter and joy from their younger years.
So much fun, so many good times,
Memories flowing like sweet nursery rhymes.

They spoke of their lives since they parted ways,
The ups and downs through the passing days.
Despite the strains and struggles they faced,
Happiness in their families was firmly placed.

Their old grudges were gone, differences dismissed,
Their bond was renewed with a brotherly kiss.
It seemed as though the years hadn't passed,
Their friendship was true and it was meant to last.

In those moments, the past was erased,
A bond so strong, it could never be replaced.
Turns out they were friends all along,
In each other's hearts, where they truly belong.

HAPPINESS KEEPS YOU SWEET. TRIALS KEEP YOU
STRONG. SORROWS KEEP YOU HUMAN. FAILURES KEEP
YOU HUMBLE. AND GOD KEEPS YOU GOING!

Sunday, November 23, 2025

Feast of Christ the King

JESUS TOUCHES THE UNTOUCHABLE

Jesus in touching the untouchable, broke a taboo,
Embracing the leper, while others withdrew.
In His love, the outcast found healing and grace,
He welcomed the shunned with a warm embrace.

Lepers lived far from the village, alone,
Their plight was one where hearts turned to stone.
But Jesus reached out where others would flee,
In His touch, He revealed true humanity.

In irony's twist, the tale takes a turn,
The leper walks free, no longer to yearn.
While Jesus, once free, now bears the weight,
Of sin and shame, as our burdens translate.

On the cross, the exchange becomes very clear,
Where we should be, it's Jesus, our King, who's there.
For our judgments and sins, He takes our place,
In His sacrifice, we find our saving grace.

So let us remember the love that He showed,
To touch and to heal, His compassion flowed.
In Jesus, the outcast finds their way home,
In His wondrous love, we are never alone.

JESUS DIED FOR YOU, KNOWING YOU MIGHT NEVER
LOVE HIM BACK. THAT'S TRUE LOVE!

Monday, November 24, 2025

THANKSGIVING'S GATHERING

We often brace for family and friends,
As Thanksgiving's gathering descends.
Every family has those who don't quite fit,
In the family plan, but they still come and sit.

With political views opposed and strong,
They argue fiercely, they go on long.
Changing subjects, is a challenging feat,
But still, they're family, a bond concrete.

They fire up quickly, emotions high,
Making us sigh and wonder why.
But in our hearts, we understand,
They are family, part of the grand plan.

We try to welcome with open arms,
To offer peace, to calm the storms.
For in hospitality, love must shine,
Even when views don't align.

So let us embrace, with kindness true,
The family who come, the old and new.
For in the spirit of Thanksgiving's call,
Love and acceptance conquers all.

GOD GAVE US OUR RELATIVES. THANK GOD WE CAN
CHOOSE OUR FRIENDS!

Tuesday, November 25, 2025

A REMINDER WHEN WE SAY THANK YOU

Even though I clutch my blanket tight,
And growl when the alarm rings, in morning light,
Thank you, Lord, that I can hear,
For many live in silence, year after year.

Even though I keep my eyes closed tight,
Against the dawn's first gentle light,
Thank you, Lord, that I can see,
For many face a world of dark eternally.

Even though the first hour's often wild,
With burnt toast and tempers riled,
Thank you, Lord, for my family near,
For many face their days alone, in silent fear.

Though our meals aren't always balanced right,
And healthy choices may be out of sight,
Thank you, Lord, for the food we share,
For many live with hunger, in need of care.

We must remind ourselves each day,
That God's the source, the guiding way.
When we say thank you, it's a reminder too,
Of the One who gives us all, in everything we do.

GOD IS SO GENEROUS THAT GOD GIVES US GRACE WE DO
NOT DESERVE, LOVE WE CANNOT COMPREHEND AND
MERCY WE CANNOT RESIST!

THANKS TO GOD FOR EVERYTHING

In the midst of the war's unyielding might,
Lincoln called for a day of light.
Amidst the bloodshed and the strife,
He urged a pause to give thanks for life.

"We've been blessed with heaven's best,
In numbers, wealth, and peaceful rest.
Yet we've forgotten the hand divine,
Thinking all these gifts were solely mine."

Enriched and strengthened, we were blind,
To the gracious hand that was so kind.
Our hearts deceived, we claimed our own,
Forgetting the seed that God had sown.

Intoxicated by success's call,
We felt no need for grace at all.
Too proud to bow, too vain to see,
That God's grace was our true decree.

So Lincoln called with solemn voice,
To acknowledge God and to rejoice.
With one heart, let the nation sing,
Thanks to God for everything.

MANY PEOPLE TURN TO GOD WHEN LIFE HAS THEM
DOWN, BUT THEY FORGET TO KEEP IN TOUCH WHEN GOD
TURNS IT ALL AROUND!!

Thursday, November 27, 2025

Thanksgiving

GIVE THANKS FOR THE BLESSINGS

When the Pilgrims gathered, their hearts full of cheer,
They had almost nothing, yet they celebrated the year.
Though hardships were plenty and comforts were few,
They feasted with gratitude, their spirits renewed.

Today we have more than those Pilgrims had,
Yet we focus on troubles, on things that are bad.
Thanksgiving's a spirit, not just one day to play,
It's a lifestyle of gratitude, living each day.

To claim we have faith, but let fear run our show,
Is to miss the whole point, to let true faith not grow.
For Thanksgiving's a call to live boldly, not hide,
In gratitude's light, let our fears be defied.

This holiday's special, no battles we cheer,
It's a moment to give thanks for the blessings so near.
Not honoring heroes or great battles won,
But giving our thanks for the good that's been done.

So let's gather together, with hearts full of grace,
Giving thanks for the blessings that light up this place.
For in gratitude's warmth, we find strength to live,
In a world full of fear, let's choose love to give.

DEAR GOD, I WANNA TAKE A MINUTE, NOT TO ASK FOR
ANYTHING FROM YOU, BUT SIMPLY TO THANK YOU FOR
ALL THAT I HAVE!

Friday, November 28, 2025

GOD KEPT A PIECE OF OUR HEART

When God formed each human heart with care,
He kept a piece up in heaven's air.
The rest God sent here to earthly ground,
To learn about love where it is often found.

We wander through our fleeting days,
Seeking love in so many ways.
Yet finding its joy is so hard to claim,
As our incomplete hearts play love's game.

For God holds back a part so dear,
A piece of our heart we can't find here.
In heaven's realm, it waits for us,
A perfect heart with love, serene and just.

In life, we search for hearts so true,
But find them cracked and split in two.
For perfect love cannot be known,
Until we claim what's heaven-grown.

One day we'll join the heavenly throng,
And find the love we've sought all along.
In God's embrace, our hearts complete,
A timeless love, will forever be sweet.

THE ONLY ONE WHO CAN TRULY SATISFY THE HUMAN
HEART IS THE ONE WHO MADE IT!

Saturday, November 29, 2025

SINCE TIME BEGAN

Since time began, God sought our devotion,
To live with values and sacred emotion.
Sometimes we listen, sometimes we stray,
But God keeps trying, each and every day.

God took human form, to win our hearts and mind,
Walking among us, so we wouldn't be blind.
In Jesus, we see forgiveness and love,
Sharing joy and courage, sent from above.

We might think we understand love's essence,
But true love shines in God's presence.
When we receive love that's unconditional and pure,
Its meaning deepens, its impact is sure.

Jesus shows us the ultimate love, divine and bright,
God's love in the flesh, a guiding light.
Seeing this example, makes the difference clear,
God's love incarnate, brings us near.

In Jesus' life, we find all that's holy and true,
Forgiveness, joy, vision, all things we should pursue.
God's effort to reach us, never fades away,
Through Jesus' love, we find our way.

IF WE DON'T TEACH OUR CHILDREN AND
GRANDCHILDREN TO FOLLOW JESUS, THE WORLD WILL
TEACH THEM NOT TO.

ADVENT IS THE TIME TO REFLECT

Advent is the time to reflect on our ways,
As we eagerly await those sacred days.
When the birth of Jesus fills us with cheer,
Yet calls us to question what we hold dear.

We shouldn't be content while others still weep,
Where hunger persists, its toll is so steep.
Beyond this season of giving, it's clear,
Compassion must guide us throughout the year.

We trust in the King born in a manger so low,
Who taught us that true worth is not in the show.
He faced the cross for speaking the truth,
To those too comfy in their worldly sleuth.

Advent invites us to seek what's right,
To challenge the darkness with a newfound light.
It's a time for change, for holding anew,
To a vision of justice, that's loving and true.

Only then does Advent make sense in our heart,
As we strive for a world where all do their part.
Holding onto hope, seeking the way,
Guided by faith as we live out each day.

WHAT A BEAUTIFUL THING IT IS TO KNOW THAT GOD'S
LOVE FOR US IS SO GREAT THAT IT HAS ABSOLUTELY NO
WAY TO BE MEASURED.

Monday, December 1, 2025

THE ADVENT WREATH

During Advent, candles are lit as a sign of hope,
Not just a ritual of piety but a way to cope.
It's a political act and a subversive stance,
A beacon of faith in the world's circumstance.

Lighting a candle is not just a religious deed,
But a prophetic act of what the world might need.
In the face of darkness, it boldly proclaims,
That God is still Lord, despite worldly claims.

Amidst the chaos that tries to dissuade,
The flicker of hope will never fade.
"All will be well," the candle declares,
A symbol of peace amid worldly affairs.

It speaks to the heart and strengthens the soul,
Reminding us that our faith can make us whole.
For every candle lit on the Advent wreath,
Shines a light of hope and a spark of belief.

So let us light candles, one by one,
A testament of faith until the night is done.
For in their glow, we find the grace to say,
That hope remains, come what may.

WRAP YOURSELF IN GOD'S LOVE ON A DAILY BASIS AND
LET IT BE YOUR GUIDE FOR EVERYTHING YOU DO!

Tuesday, December 2, 2025

SHOULD YOU FIND IT HARD TO SLEEP TONIGHT

Should you find it hard to sleep tonight,
Think of those with no bed in sight.
Remember the family without a place,
Finding shelter in a homeless space.

Should you find yourself stuck in traffic's snare,
Think of those who don't drive anywhere.
To many, cars are a privilege unknown,
With dreams of journeys they've never flown.

Should you have a rough day at your work,
Think of those who are waiting for a spark.
For months they've searched without success,
Yet their spirits refuse to regress.

Should you despair over a love's lost song,
Think of those who've never belonged.
Who've never felt love's warm embrace,
Or shared in its tender, sweet grace.

In every struggle, a lesson to learn,
A deeper compassion to discern.
Count your blessings, however small,
And find the strength to rise above it all.

SLEEP DOESN'T HELP IF IT'S YOUR SOUL THAT IS TIRED!

WHERE PRAYER AND ACTION MEET

In life, where prayer and action meet,
Integrity must always guide our feet.
For words alone, like hollow cries,
Often fall short of truth, becoming lies.

To live by whims, neglecting grace,
Will leave our prayers in a barren space.
Yet morals void of prayer's embrace,
Can harden hearts and slow our pace.

In balance lies the path we seek,
Where prayer and action truly speak.
But lip service can lead us astray,
When truth and hearts both slip away.

Words are cheap in this digital age,
Where hollow claims can fill the page.
Yet in the quiet, souls will thirst,
For righteousness, it's a hunger first.

Let actions mirror the prayers we say,
With honesty to light our way.
For only then can we aspire,
To walk with God as we climb higher.

GOD WORKS THROUGH A RESTED MIND AND AN OPEN
HEART!

Thursday, December 4, 2025

MORAL SOCIETIES STAND SO TALL

Moral societies stand so tall,
With honesty and truth for all.
Integrity that's in every heart,
Is where prosperity can start.

In faith and honor, trust we see,
The pillars of community.
A deep belief in laws and grace,
Uplifts and binds the human race.

Great societies bloom in peace,
Where love and harmony increase.
Respect for others, hand in hand,
Builds up a just and noble land.

Beyond ourselves, we look above,
To Someone great, a God of love.
In faith we find a common ground,
Where hope and justice do abound.

So study well the past and know,
That morals guide and help us grow.
A prosperous society,
Is one that holds integrity.

GOD IS, AND WILL ALWAYS BE, GREATER THAN YOUR
CIRCUMSTANCES!

TAKE THE TIME TO STEP ASIDE

When crowds got close, Jesus slipped away,
To pray and find His strength in God each day.
In quiet moments, his purpose was clear,
His path was shown, His heart was sincere.

We need to learn to close the door,
To find the peace we're longing for.
In solitude, we find our way,
To hear what God would have us say.

Without this time to pause and rest,
Our minds can stray from what is best.
The load we bear might cause us harm,
Unless we seek God's healing calm.

In stress and strain, we lose our aim,
And life can seem a reckless game.
But when we turn to God above,
We realign with truth and love.

So take the time to step aside,
In God's embrace, let peace abide.
For only then can we fulfill,
The purpose of His perfect will.

LIFE WITHOUT GOD IS LIKE AN UNSHARPENED
PENCIL…..IT HAS NO POINT!

Saturday, December 6, 2025

WE LIVE IN TWO DIFFERENT WORLDS

Every day we are aware of two different worlds,
Store windows adorned with gifts and pearls,
While outside someone rings a Salvation Army bell,
Amidst the splendor, there's a tale of need to tell.

TV commercials show SUV's so grand,
Followed by news of children across the land,
Homeless and starving, their plight is real,
A stark reminder of wounds we must heal.

In human history, it's hard to see,
How these two worlds can ever be free,
But Jesus came, with healing grace,
Uniting hearts, in every place.

He healed the rich, he healed the poor,
The blind, the lame, and so much more.
Through spiritual healing, love unfurled,
Jesus bridged the gap between two worlds.

This Advent let us follow in His way,
Bringing hope and light each day.
For in acts of love, both great and small,
We bring together, one and all.

PAY ATTENTION TO YOUR DREAMS, THEY ARE YOUR
LETTERS FROM GOD!

Sunday, December 7, 2025

JOHN THE BAPTIST

John the Baptist speaks with God's own voice,
His words invite, they don't coerce.
His foretelling of what will soon take place,
By calling hearts to a higher grace.

His words radiate love, not push us away,
With gentle strength, they guide the way.
His voice may upset, yet also draw,
Revealing truths that are without a flaw.

Challenging us to nobler heights,
John shines a path with purest lights.
His words, both solace and demand,
Inspire us all to take a stand.

John beckons us to what's true and right,
To love more deeply, to shine more bright.
In his message, we clearly see,
A glimpse of the divine prophecy.

For in his call, we recognize,
The voice of God, the prophet's ties.
A challenge, yet a sweet embrace,
Guiding us to God's own grace.

GOD LOVES WITH A GREAT LOVE THE PERSON WHOSE
HEART IS BURSTING WITH A PASSION FOR THE
IMPOSSIBLE!

Monday, December 8, 2025

Mary's Immaculate Conception

MARY LOOKED UPWARD

Mary looked back and saw a surprise,
A life unexpected, before her eyes.
The angel came with news divine,
That she'd bear a Savior, by God's design.

Mary looked inward and joyfully cried,
"Great things for me, God has supplied."
Through every challenge and joyful stride,
God's surprises filled her with pride.

Mary looked forward, her faith so strong,
Raising Jesus, where she belonged.
Through life, death, and resurrection's grace,
She nurtured God's love, His gentle embrace.

Mary looked upward, with a faith so pure,
Connected with God, her path was secure.
Giving God her address, her soul to find,
In trust and love, her heart was aligned.

God said to Mary, "Work with Me,
As instruments of love, we'll be."
Let us, like Mary, in faith and trust,
Work with God, as instruments of the just.

I AM NOT IN CONTROL, BUT, LIKE MARY, I AM DEEPLY
LOVED BY THE ONE WHO IS!

Tuesday, December 9, 2025

ADVENT SPEAKS OF A LONGING DEEP

Advent speaks of a longing deep,
A yearning that our hearts do keep.
In daily strife and tears we find,
A hope that heals our aching mind.

Incompleteness, and our daily grind,
Brings a closer peace we long to find.
Each tear we shed, each pain we bear,
Prepares our way with tender care.

Frustration teaches love and grace,
Each longing leads to a sacred place.
In every groan of our despair,
A prayer is born, a whispered care.

Preparing not with lights and cheer,
But with a heart that draws Him near.
To yearn, to pray, to deeply feel,
Creating inner space for Christ to heal.

This season calls us to expand,
Our hearts and minds to understand.
In every act, a womb is made,
Within which Christ's birth will never fade.

"NORMAL" IS NOT COMING BACK. JESUS IS!

Wednesday, December 10, 2025

MISSING THE WONDER ON DISPLAY

How many gaze at screens all day,
And miss the wonders on display?
The lilies bloom with grace and light,
Yet go unseen both day and night.

Our culture chases wealth and gain,
In this pursuit, we miss the rain.
The fragile miracles unfold,
Their stories lost, their beauty untold.

Rainbows arc across the sky,
While geese in formation fly.
Yet eyes are fixed on what's unreal,
Ignoring nature's grand appeal.

In wildflowers and morning dew,
God's presence whispers, fresh and true.
But do we see the hand that made,
This world where miracles cascade?

Let hearts awaken, eyes behold,
The treasures of the world unfold.
In every leaf and petal bright,
Find God's love in its purest light.

IF GOD HOLDS THE UNIVERSE TOGETHER, GOD IS
HOLDING YOUR WORLD TOGETHER AS WELL!

Thursday, December 11, 2025

IN LIFE'S SLOW MARCH WE GROW SO COLD

In life's slow march we grow so cold,
Our hearts like stones, our spirits old.
We age unseen, like greying hair,
Until a photo shows the wear.

Once eager, spontaneous, and free,
Now hard and bitter, can't you see?
Hospitality, joy, they fade away,
Replaced by shadows, dull and gray.

We mirror gaze, we think we're the same,
But old snapshots reveal the shame.
Compassion lost, joy turned to dust,
In life's harsh grind, we lose our trust.

A prayer for hearts to soften and mend,
To find the joy we once did tend.
Moments of grace, to bring us back,
To love, to laugh, to find the track.

"Pray always," is a call to keep,
Even when it's in silence deep.
For in those moments, hearts can heal,
And regain the childlike joy we once did feel.

YOU CAN'T EMBRACE GOD'S FORGIVENESS IF YOU ARE
SO BUSY CLINGING TO PAST WOUNDS AND NURSING OLD
GRUDGES!

Friday, December 12, 2025

UNAWARE OF MIRACLES BORN

We live our long, worn days in shade,
In barren cold, our spirits fade.
Unaware of miracles born,
In winter's grasp, our souls forlorn.

Yet sudden light, the surprise of life,
Can lift our gaze from daily strife.
To see a growth so quiet, so true,
Inside our hearts, a stunning view.

Like frost on windows, beauty clear,
Beyond life's fragments, hope draws near.
Not lost as deeply as we thought,
In coldest times, new life was wrought.

When shadows linger, and seem to stay,
Inside, our spirits find their way.
Unseen, unheard, they quietly bloom,
Bringing light to winter's gloom.

So, in the dark, we find our grace,
In silent growth, our resting place.
Though days feel worn, and nights are long,
Within us stirs a hopeful song.

EVERYDAY GOD THINKS OF YOU. EVERY HOUR GOD
LOOKS AFTER YOU. EVERY MINUTE GOD CARES FOR
YOU, BECAUSE EVERY SECOND GOD LOVES YOU!

Saturday, December 13, 2025

ADVENT IS A TIME TO LOOK WITHIN

Advent is a time of stories, of Jesus' birth so dear,
But also a time to look within, to see ourselves clear.
We shouldn't be comfortable with hunger near our door,
For their pain lasts longer than the season's festive lore.

We shouldn't be at ease while wars claim countless lives,
Or ignore the suffering that in our midst survives.
Generosity in holidays should stretch throughout the year,
To soothe the cries of those we hold so near.

The alternative is trusting in a King born in a trough,
Who teaches us to care for all, not to shrug or scoff.
For people who trust in God, status means so little,
Christ showed love's vast power, born in a place so brittle.

He was strung upon a cross for truths that pierced the heart,
Speaking to a world content, that needed a fresh start.
So in this Advent season, let's not seek comfort's call,
But strive to make a difference, with love and care for all.

Let's open up our hearts, extend a helping hand,
To those who are in need, across this troubled land.
For in each act of kindness, in every selfless deed,
We honor the spirit of Christ, and plant a hopeful seed.

ARE YOU PART OF THE INN CROWD, OR ARE YOU ONE OF
THE STABLE FEW!

Sunday, December 14, 2025

WE LIGHT ADVENT CANDLES IN THE NIGHT

We light Advent candles in the night,
Not swayed by the news, but for their Light.
A deeper truth, beyond our fear,
That God exists, and God is near.

The center holds, though all seems wrong,
God's love and power remain so strong.
He rules the stars, the earth, the skies,
And brings new life where darkness dies.

We light these flames with hope renewed,
That love and peace will be pursued.
For God, who formed the world with grace,
Has promised joy to every place.

The Lord of all, both just and kind,
Will heal the earth and free the blind.
His kingdom comes, we know it's true,
A world made whole, for me, for you.

So let these candles brightly burn,
As we await Christ's great return.
In every flame, a hope is cast,
God's love will reign, the storm will pass.

THE JESUS INSIDE ME IS STRONGER THAN THE
DARKNESS THAT THREATENS TO OVERTAKE ME!

THE TREES SPOKE SILENTLY

In fall, I watched the leaves descend,
As branches reached where skies extend.
With leaves all gone, they still aspire,
Toward heaven's help, their faith entire.

When winter's snow and winds did press,
The branches bent, but did not stress.
They kept their stance, no matter the strain,
In patient faith, through cold and pain.

In spring, the trees spoke silently,
"Look up, our help comes faithfully."
With buds and blooms, their branches said,
"God's promise kept, we're always fed."

They praised with or without their leaves,
In patient wait, their heart believes.
For in their reach, they show their trust,
That from above comes all that's just.

God gives not always what we plea,
But what we need, that we might live free.
Through all the seasons, hold on tight,
His promise keeps us through the night.

SOME OF THE BEST THINGS JESUS WILL DO IN YOUR LIFE
WON'T BE ON YOUR SCHEDULE!

Tuesday, December 16, 2025

THE BREAD OF LIFE

When you chase the hunger for fleeting things,
Dissatisfaction is all it brings.
The more you seek, the more you crave,
Deeper into the hole you pave.

A bigger slice of wealth or fame,
Leaves you empty, just the same.
Urges fed, yet never full,
Your soul's left feeling cold and dull.

In a world where consuming reigns,
People work through endless pains.
Accumulating what won't last,
In a cycle, that's spinning fast.

Jesus spoke, "I am the Bread of Life,"
A call to end this endless strife.
True fulfillment is found in Him,
Not in riches or a fleeting whim.

So turn from chasing worldly gain,
Seek the bread that ends all pain.
In His words, find peace and light,
In His love, discover your appetite.

OUR GOD IS THE GOD OF THE UNEXPECTED. FEW THINGS
COULD BE MORE UNEXPECTED THAN THE KING OF
HEAVEN BEING BORN IN A STABLE!

Wednesday, December 17, 2025

WHEN A CHILD IS BORN

When a child is born, they find their place,
In a mother's arms, in a warm embrace.
Without her care, they'd face the cold,
Unready for the world, too young, too bold.

A mother's touch can ease the strife,
Her tenderness can shape a life.
Though birth brings trauma, it doesn't last,
Her love and patience heal the past.

With gentle hands and soothing voice,
She makes the world a place to rejoice.
From birth to growth, a wondrous quest,
Her guidance turns it to the best.

God is our mother, ever more kind,
In death's embrace, true peace we find.
Through life to death, a sacred path,
Held by His love, we feel no wrath.

As in our infancy, tenderly cared,
So in death's transition, we're prepared.
Not rough, but gentle, are His ways,
Leading us to our eternal days.

A BABY'S SMILE IS A SPECIAL GIFT FROM GOD!

Thursday, December 18, 2025

JESUS IS THE HINGE OF HISTORY'S DOOR

The doorways of life on hinges swing,
On crucial matters, they often cling.
Christmas depends on Christ's birth, you see,
Yet society ever forgets His legacy.

Democracy relies on respect for all,
Rights taken for granted, ignored in the call.
Christmas, the Church, and schools we adore,
Hinge on values we must not ignore.

God's love reveals blessings so bright,
Through acts of kindness, we see the light.
The greatest gift is love's embrace,
Showing us goodness in every place.

Jesus, the hinge of history's door,
Guides us to love and so much more.
For wise are those who truly see,
Life's hinges bring unity and harmony.

Let us cherish the hinges of life,
Appreciate them amidst the strife.
For through these hinges, doors open wide,
Leading us forward with love as our guide.

EACH OF US IS AN INNKEEPER WHO DECIDES IF THERE IS
ROOM FOR JESUS IN OUR HEART!

EMMANUEL'S LOVE IS EVER NIGH

Emmanuel means, "God with us," each day,
Not just in dreams or when we kneel to pray.
He walks beside us in mundane affairs,
In bustling mornings and daily cares.

He's present in the clinics where pain may dwell,
In nursing homes, where life's tales do swell.
In lonely rooms when we pack away,
The festive trinkets of our holiday's display.

When friendships falter and calls don't arrive,
He's there to remind us that hope is alive.
In moments of anger, when tears overflow,
Emmanuel whispers, "I'm with you, you know."

With eyes so gentle, he meets our gaze,
Not just in laughter, but in tearful daze.
In anger or doubt, when we turn away,
His love never falters, it's here to stay.

So when you feel lost, remember the call,
His name tells the truth: He's with us through it all.
In every heartbeat, in every sigh,
Emmanuel's love is ever nigh.

JESUS IS THE ONLY GIFT THAT PERFECTLY FITS THE SIZE
OF YOUR HEART!

THE SMALL CHILD OF BETHLEHEM

The small child of Bethlehem, humble and small,
The young man of Nazareth, unnoticed by all,
The preacher rejected, the man on the cross,
He asks for my focus, despite the world's gloss.

In the midst of a world full of noise and acclaim,
Where promises abound but seldom sustain,
The work of salvation quietly unfolds,
A truth often missed in the stories we're told.

Amidst the shouting, the world's grand parade,
Lies the promise of life that never will fade.
Hidden in the shoot from Jesse's old root,
A hope for the future that takes a silent root.

In the overlooked places, where few choose to see,
Sprouts the promise of peace and true harmony.
A quiet reminder that greatness can start
In the simplest of places, as within a pure heart.

So let us give heed to the quiet and small,
For in their gentle whisper, we hear our call.
To seek out the promise where it humbly grows,
And discover salvation despite what the world throws.

WE MUST NOT MEASURE GREATNESS FROM THE
MANSION DOWN, BUT FROM THE MANGER UP!

Sunday, December 21, 2025

ADVENT IS A JOURNEY

Advent is a journey, or so we believe,
A path we must take, the world to leave.
But the journey's not ours, we're not in command,
It's God's trip to us, as He takes our hand.

To Bethlehem's village, through time we dream,
A journey not ours, though it may well seem.
We prepare for His coming, our hearts to align,
For God's trip to us, is a gift so divine.

The road is not ours, it's His to traverse,
Through all of creation, God's loving universe.
We ready ourselves to receive His grace,
As God journeys to us, in this sacred space.

No map we must follow, no path to prepare,
For God's journey to us is beyond compare.
In Advent's sweet season, let hearts be aware,
That God travels to us, our souls to repair.

So in this season, let us prepare,
For the journey of God, beyond all compare.
In the silence and stillness, we'll find our way,
As God comes to us, on this holy day.

SUDDENLY I REALIZED THAT EVERY SINGLE THING IN
MY LIFE IS FLEETING, AND ONLY GOD IS ETERNAL.

Monday, December 22, 2025

THE JOY AND SORROW OF CHRISTMAS

Each year it's harder to find the cheer,
The mood of Christmas we once held dear.
Memories warm us, from days gone by,
When lights and carols made spirits fly.

As children, Christmas brought pure delight,
Anticipation glowed ever so bright.
Now, as adults, the joy seems thin,
Commercial excess, where to begin?

Personal tragedies, we've faced our share,
Lost health, lost time, loved ones not there.
Tired and frustrated, hearts heavy with grief,
How do we find the Christmas belief?

Christmas asks us to embrace,
Joy and sorrow, in this space.
Christ's birth is a challenge to see,
Love and pain in harmony.

So let us find the light within,
Despite the noise, despite the din.
God is with us, every day,
In our hearts, He'll always stay.

A THOUSAND TIMES IN HISTORY A BABY BECOMES A
KING. BUT ONLY ONCE IN HISTORY DID A KING BECOME
A BABY!

Tuesday, December 23, 2025

OUR CHRISTMAS LIGHTS

Our Christmas lights, so small and bright,
Are symbols of our faith's pure light.
In a world where darkness seems to reign,
They shine as hope amid the pain.

We see a world in dark distress,
Where countless souls are dispossessed.
What use is faith, in lights so small,
When shadows loom and tempests call?

With wars and hunger, pain and strife,
Our lights seem weak against such life.
But in their glow, a truth we find,
That darkness cannot blind the mind.

For prayer is needed most, they say,
When all seems lost, when hope's away.
Our lights declare, both far and near,
That Christ's own love will conquer fear.

So let them shine, each tiny spark,
A beacon in the world so dark.
For in these lights, our faith is shown,
That in Christ's love, we're not alone.

BABIES ARE BITS OF STARDUST BLOWN FROM THE HAND
OF GOD!

Wednesday, December 24, 2025

Christmas Eve

CHRIST'S CRY WHISPERS SOFTLY

Christ's Cry is often a gentle, soft sound,
Reminding us that life's worth can be found.
In our everyday moments, through trials and peace,
Christ's Cry whispers softly, offering us release.

Christ's Cry is sometimes a piercing, loud call,
To open our hearts and to challenge us all.
To listen with care, beyond gossip and noise,
To the truth that awaits when we make the right choice.

Christ's Cry is found in the pain we conceal,
Injustice and hurt that we struggle to heal.
It calls for the brave to uncover what's wrong,
To stand for the weak and to help them be strong.

Christ's Cry beckons us to unite and embrace,
To bridge every gap with love's gentle grace.
In families, communities, nations, and lands,
To strive for a unity that love understands.

Christ's Cry is the call of a lost, lonely soul,
Forgotten by many but known by the Whole.
It rises to heaven, a melody so sweet,
Where angels and loved ones in harmony meet.

CHRISTMAS BEGAN IN THE HEART OF GOD. IT IS ONLY
COMPLETE WHEN IT REACHES YOUR HEART AND MINE!

Thursday, December 25, 2025

Christmas Day

A CHORUS OF ANGELS SANG IN THE NIGHT

It is a tale that always stretches our mind,
Of God in flesh, with humankind entwined.
In a humble town, God chose to appear,
In a place overlooked, yet held so dear.

Who but God would choose such a way,
In a small village, so hidden away?
Born to a mother, humble and meek,
In a world where virtue seemed so weak.

The birth was announced, not to the grand,
But to shepherds in fields, such a lowly band.
A chorus of angels sang in the night,
Proclaiming the gift of the holy light.

This story calls for faith-filled eyes,
To see beyond what the world denies.
It beckons us to see anew,
The vision that only the faithful knew.

A challenge to dream beyond what is seen,
To envision a world where grace can convene.
In this humble birth, a hope is unfurled,
God's love embracing the whole wide world.

JESUS TOOK HIS PLACE IN A MANGER SO YOU MIGHT
HAVE A PLACE IN HEAVEN!

GOD IN INFANT FORM

Why would God descend in infant form,
Not as a force, a superhuman storm?
The world in need, with hearts so direly torn,
Received a child, in a humble stable born.

Not sweetness pure, nor innocence so bright,
But power found in helplessness, the light.
In a manger low and a cross so stark and bare,
The message clear: true strength lies not in despair.

Vulnerability is, the path to life,
Not might nor force, nor conquering in strife.
For in the weak, the kingdom finds its place,
A child's helplessness, a true gift of grace.

In children's eyes, the kingdom's way is revealed,
Not in power gained, but in tender hearts unsealed.
For helplessness, not strength, will open doors,
And life begins where weakness first implores.

A superman would only bring more strife,
But in a child, we find the source of life.
God sent a baby, gentle, small, and true,
For in that pure love, our healing does ensue.

PEACE ON EARTH WILL COME TO STAY WHEN WE LIVE
CHRISTMAS EVERYDAY!

Saturday, December 27, 2025

BLESSED ARE THEY WHO FIND CHRISTMAS

Blessed are they who find Christmas in a story old,
Of a babe in Bethlehem, resting in a manger cold.
To them, a little child brings hope anew,
A promise of peace in a world askew.

Blessed are they who find Christmas in the star so bright,
Their lives reflect its beauty and its light.
Guided by its glow, they walk a path so clear,
Sharing love and joy, spreading Christmas cheer.

Blessed are they who find Christmas in giving,
With hearts so full, their joy is found in living.
They share the gladness of shepherds and wise men,
Bringing happiness to others, again and again.

Blessed are they who find Christmas in the music's rhyme,
With songs of joy that echo throughout time.
A melody of hope ever singing in their hearts,
A symphony of love that never departs.

Blessed are they who find Christmas in the Prince of Peace,
Ever striving to help his message increase.
Bringing peace on earth, good will to men,
Truly blessed are they, time and again.

WHAT DO I PROFIT IF JESUS IS BORN IN THOUSANDS OF
PLACES ALL OVER THE WORLD, BUT JESUS IS NOT BORN
IN MY OWN HEART?

Sunday, December 28, 2025

Holy Family Sunday

CHRISTMAS REVEALS GOD'S HUMBLE WAY

Christmas reveals God's humble way,
In ordinary life, He's here to stay.
No need for miracles or sights so grand,
In daily moments, God takes our hand.

Not in the spectacle or the grand display,
But in our kitchens, where we pray.
At our tables, in our wounds so deep,
In each other's faces, His presence we keep.

When Jesus walked the earth, few could see,
The look of a Messiah in His simplicity.
They sought a king, all filled with might,
But found a man, gentle and slight.

Born in a stable, meek and mild,
He didn't fit the image they'd compiled.
No forceful power, just love and grace,
In Him was God's very ordinary face.

So, find Christmas in the simple, the small,
In the quiet moments, where God embraces all.
For God is found at home in the everyday,
In our humble lives, He'll always stay.

BECAUSE OF THE BIRTH OF JESUS, WE HAVE GOD'S JOY
IN OUR BLOOD!

Monday, December 29, 2025

WE GIVE BIRTH TO JESUS

How do you prove that God exists?
Not through experiments or rational twists.
God's presence in the world we feel,
Gestated like Mary, oh so real.

Mary, not just an icon to admire,
But a pattern of how God's love we inspire.
Through charity, joy, and peace we find,
God's word in us, a birth aligned.

Pregnant with patience, goodness, and faith,
We bear the divine, in every breath.
Morning sickness of soul we bear,
Bringing forth love, with utmost care.

With groans of flesh, in pain and strife,
We give birth to Jesus, we bring Him to life.
Nursing the Christ in acts so kind,
God's incarnation, all intertwined.

Years we spend, coaxing love to grow,
In every heart, let Jesus show.
For that's the way God takes on form,
In human lives, love is reborn.

IT IS CHRISTMAS EVERY TIME YOU LET GOD LOVE
OTHERS THROUGH YOU!

PERHAPS JESUS LOVED TO DANCE

Perhaps Jesus loved to dance, such joy in His heart,
Born at a party, that's where celebrations start.
With heavenly light and the angels' song,
With gifts from afar, the dance was long.

His favorite miracle, turning water to wine,
Not vinegar, but something so divine.
Feeding thousands with one boy's meal,
His love and care, was always real.

He spoke of kings and banquets grand,
And a father's joy, with an open hand.
A wayward son was welcomed back home,
Love and forgiveness, was widely known.

After His return, He served a fish barbecue,
On the shore, a team picnic was in full view.
From a happy place, He did come,
To a joyous place, He'd return home.

"Why do you worry?" He'd gently ask,
"See the flowers, in beauty they bask.
If God clothes them in such array,
Will He not care for you, each day?"

IF YOU KEEP CHRIST IN YOUR HEART, CHRISTMAS WILL
NEVER END!

Wednesday, December 31, 2025

New Year's Eve

AS ONE YEAR ENDS, ANOTHER STARTS

As one year ends, another starts,
Reflective minds and sobering hearts.
Another year has come and gone,
With memories, at both dusk and dawn.

Maybe someone dear has died,
Or a newborn brought you joy inside.
Perhaps new paths you've dared to tread,
Graduated, moved or are newlywed.

It could be work that's come to an end,
Or health restored by medicine's friend.
Maybe frustration held its sway,
Or fulfillment brightened every day.

A paradox of joy and pain,
Growth and loss, sunshine and rain.
Death and love, both side by side,
Life's a rollercoaster ride.

Bethlehems and Calvaries blend,
Joy and sorrow, without end.
As Christians, we hope to see,
In all these things, life's mystery.

WHEN YOU FIX YOUR THOUGHTS ON THE BIRTH OF
JESUS, GOD FIXES YOUR THOUGHTS!

WITH GRATITUDE

I especially give thanks to Tim Veach, the Founder of:
Designs for Success
Web Designs Without Limits

Tim Veach has been a dear friend and colleague of mine for forty years in all of my many endeavors. Tim has been invaluable to me in countless ways with his support, his technical ability, his digital expertise, his marketing skills, and his refinement of the cover of this book. Tim introduced me to the Digital Age thirty years ago, getting me my first Toshiba laptop. He has guided my fingers on the keyboard ever since. I value his great patience with me and all that he has taught me over the years. Without Tim's great assistance, this book would not have been possible.

ABOUT THE AUTHOR

Medard Laz is a Roman Catholic priest of the Archdiocese of Chicago. He was ordained a priest in 1969 and has served in six parishes in Chicagoland and six parishes in southeast Florida. He is the founding pastor of Holy Family Parish Community in Inverness, Illinois. Laz is the author of nine books on marriage and family life, including the best-selling , *Love Adds a Little Chocolate.*

Medard is the founder of *Joyful Again!*, a weekend retreat for widows and widowers to help them with their grief. He co-founded *Rainbows for All Children*, a 15-week program for children who have suffered a life-altering event as a result of death, divorce, a hurricane or a mass-shooting. Over four million children have attended in thirteen countries.

Laz founded *Hearts for Humanity* and co-founded *Angels in Action* to help educate and feed children and young adults in Haiti and the Dominican Republic. He has worked with *Food for the Poor* to help build schools, hospitals and homes in Haiti.

Med contributes to his website and podcast, *TreatsfortheSoul.org* on a daily basis where he provides his *Daily Treats* and *Weekly Messages* to promote spiritual growth and a closer relationship with Jesus.

Fr. Medard Laz lives and ministers locally and around the world from his home in Fort Lauderdale, Florida.